REED CONCISE GUIDE

LILIES
of Australia

INCLUDING THEIR RELATIVES AND LOOKALIKES

David L Jones

First published in 2024 by Reed New Holland Publishers
Sydney

Level 1, 178 Fox Valley Road, Wahroonga, NSW 2076, Australia

newhollandpublishers.com

A record of this book is held at the National Library of Australia.

ISBN 978 1 76079 617 4

Managing Director: Fiona Schultz
Publisher and Project Editor: Simon Papps
Designer: Andrew Davies
Production Director: Arlene Gippert

Printed in China

10 9 8 7 6 5 4 3 2 1

Keep up with Reed New Holland
and New Holland Publishers

ReedNewHolland

@NewHollandPublishers and @ReedNewHolland

Front cover: *Thelionema caespitosum*

Page 1: *Anigozanthos preissii.*

Page 3: Colony of *Crinum luteolum.*

Back cover: *Burchardia rosea,* C. French

CONTENTS

Opposite page: *Bulbine crassa*.

Wurmbea dioica.

INTRODUCTION

The plants included in this book are commonly referred to by botanists as 'petaloid monocots.' Some authors also call them 'lilioid monocots' because of their similarity to lilies. Visitors to the bush, however, might know them better under such familiar names as irises, milkmaids, squills, nancies, stars, bloodroots, Christmas bells, leeks, flags, cottonheads, cat's paws, kangaroo paws, aroids and various types of lilies. This small book contains 180 species of Australian native petaloid monocots in 52 genera, a reasonable sample of the species found in this remarkable continent. Most of the photos are mine, taken during my travels while chasing orchids, but I have also sought others from colleagues to extend the coverage. My thanks to David Banks for his shots of *Blandfordia cunninghamii*; Bob Bates for *Calostemma abdicatum, Crinum flaccidum, C. luteolum* and *Wurmbea citrina*; Trevor Blake for *Wurmbea centralis*; Christopher French for *Burchardia rosea, Chamaexeros serra, Wurmbea drummondii, W. inflata, W. murchisoniana* and *W. tubulosa*; Sandie Jones for *Crinum pedunculatum*; Stephen van Leeuwin for *Wurmbea saccata*; Russell Barrett for *Asparagus racemosus, Proiphys kimberleyensis* and *Thysanotus elatior*, and Hans and Mark Wapstra for *Isophysis tasmanica*.

Numbers: There are about 70,000 species of monocots in the world, with a 'guesstimate' placing many thousands in Australia, most of which are endemic. The largest family of monocots is the Orchidaceae with c. 20,000 species (c.1,700 spp. in Australia). Grasses, some 12,000 spp. (c.1,320 spp. in Australia), provide not only vital food for the world's herbivores but also a major contribution to the world's economy. Other distinctive monocots include palms, pandans, bamboos, bromeliads, gingers, bananas, reeds, rushes, sedges, aroids and many aquatics.

Lily names: The text of this book includes at least one common name for each species as well as a designated binomial name that consists of a genus name and species epithet. For example, the common name Christmas Bells is associated with the botanical name *Blandfordia grandiflora*, with *Blandfordia* being the name of the genus and *grandiflora* the species name. Botanically, binomial names are more accurately applied than common names, which often arise from general usage or popularity. A species can have several common names but only a single accurate binomial name.

The common names used in this book are those that are widely adopted or commonly accepted.

Arrangement of species: The lilies, lily relatives and lily lookalikes included in this book are arranged alphabetically by their botanical names within their plant family and the plant families are arranged alphabetically throughout the text. The family placement of genera used in this book is based on the results of recent molecular-based genetic studies and may cause some confusion to readers since the family placement used here will often differ from traditional concepts. For example, most monocot genera included in Volume 45 of *Flora of Australia*, published in 1987, were assigned to the family Liliaceae but, following recent genetic studies, today no native Australian genera are placed in Liliaceae.

Monocotyledons: The lilies and their relatives, which are part of the major group of plants known as monocotyledons (also known as monocots), are linked together by shared features found in the structure of their plants and flowers. Monocotyledons are an important group of plants that can be recognised by a set of morphological features, the main ones being a single seed leaf (cotyledon), herbaceous habit of growth, narrow leaves with a basal sheath and parallel venation, and flowers with segments in multiples of three. These features are used in combination to identify a monocotyledon but no feature on its own is distinctive for the group.

The root system that develops from the monocot seedling is typically short-lived and is replaced by a series of adventitious roots which arise over time from the stem and shoots. Monocots also have specialised subterranean growths such as rhizomes and

Doryanthes palmeri.

stolons which allow the plants to spread into new areas. Many native species die back to subterranean storage organs, such as fleshy roots, thickened stems, tubers, corms and bulbs to avoid prolonged periods of heat and dryness. These storage organs contain water and nutrients for the survival of the plant in hard times. Known as resprouters, these species produce new growth with the advent of substantial rains and more congenial conditions. The stems of monocots lack a cambial layer and therefore cannot develop secondary thickening in the usual way of woody trees, although larger woody monocots such as palms and pandans have developed a specialised form of secondary thickening which allows them to grow larger. Monocot leaves are typically narrow with parallel venation, although a few specialised species have leaves with a broad blade and reticulate venation which branches in a

Pauridia vaginata.

network. Many species have a specialised sheathing base which attaches the leaf to the stem. Very few have a petiole.

The outer whorl of the petal-like structures in a monocot flower is analogous to the sepals of a dicotyledon flower and the inner whorl is analogous to petals. Often the sepals and petals of petaloid monocots are very similar in size, shape and colour and are then referred to as tepals. The inner whorl of tepals (petals) is commonly thin textured or even membranous and the flowers frequently short-lived (fugacious), usually lasting less than a day and often withering a few hours after opening in the morning. Petaloid monocot flowers are often showy, colourful and sweetly perfumed to attract insects for pollination. Many also have specialised tubular anthers with an apical opening to attract buzz-pollinating native bees to the flowers. Specialised hairs on the staminal filaments of some other species also play a similar role of insect attraction. A few native species have small flowers enclosed in colourful bracts which take over the role of pollinator attraction (*Johnsonia* is an example).

Abbreviations used in the text:

AKA	also known as.
c.	circa, approximately
Dec, Jan, Feb, etc	December, January, February, etc
E(e)	east
Indon.	Indonesia
infl.	inflorescence
Is.	island(s)
N(n)	north
NCal	New Caledonia
NG	New Guinea
NSW	New South Wales
NT	Northern Territory
occas.	occasional(ly)
PKA	previously known as
Qld	Queensland
Ra.	ranges
SA	South Australia
S(s)	south
sp.	species singular
spp.	species plural
Tas	Tasmania
tlnds.	tablelands
Vic	Victoria
W(w)	west
WA	Western Australia

Alphabetical overview of genera included in this book

Agrostocrinum (Asphodelaceae): 2 spp. and 1 subsp., endemic in WA. Perennial, resprouting tufting lilies with a rhizome. Roots tuberous. Aerial stems annual. Leaves annual, sword shaped. Infl. branched. Flowers bisexual, short-lived (hours). Tepals subequal, twisting after flowering. Stamens 6. Fruit a 3-lobed globose capsule.

Alania (Boryaceae): Monotypic genus endemic in NSW.

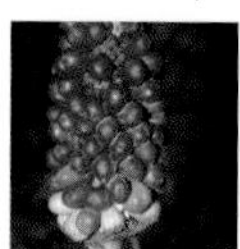

Amorphophallus (Araceae): 170 spp., 2 in Aust., neither endemic, also 1 undescribed; NG, Africa, Asia, Oceania. Deciduous, resprouting cormous aroids. Leaf usually single. Petiole often mottled. Blades compoundly divided. Infl. arising before leaves, *Arum*-like, mostly solitary, fragrant or smelly. Spathe narrow to broad, flag-like, often black/purple. Flowers unisexual, tiny, on a fleshy spadix with separate male and female zones. Fruit a berry.

Anigozanthos (Haemodoraceae): 11 spp. endemic in WA. Perennial clumping herbs with short stems. Leaves flat or nearly terete. Infl. simple or branched, often one-sided. Flowers zygomorphic, bisexual, tubular with spreading lobes, covered with colourful woolly hairs. Stamens 6, protruding like claws. Fruit a capsule. NOTES: Distinctive, colourful lily-relatives prominent in the WA flora. Spectacular floral displays after fire.

Arthropodium (Asparagaceae): 18 spp., 13 in Aust., some unnamed; NZ, NCal., Madagascar. Evergreen or resprouting lilies with tuberous roots. Leaves often short-lived. Infl. erect/arching, raceme/panicle. Flowers bisexual, often nodding, short-lived (hours). Tepals 6. Sepals narrower than petals. Filaments of some adorned with a prominent brush of spreading hairs. Fruit a capsule. NOTES: Includes *Dichopogon* spp. Roots and flowers of many spp. are edible.

Asparagus (Asparagaceae): 100 spp., mainly Africa, Asia, 1 widespread sp. extending to Aust. Perennial shrubby or climbing lilies with tuberous roots. Branchlets leaf-like. Leaves small, scale-like, occas. with spines. Flowers bisexual, single or clusters. Tepals 6, equal. Stamens 6. Fruit a red/orange/ black berry. NOTES: Roots and young shoots edible.

Blancoa (Haemodoraceae): Monotypic genus endemic in WA.

Borya (Boryaceae) 12 spp. all endemic in Aust. Perennials forming domed clumps or spreading by rhizomes. Stems branched, occas. with stilt roots. Leaves very narrow, stiff, crowded, sharply pointed. Flowers small, white/cream, in clusters atop slender scapes. Perianth tubular with 6 spreading lobes. Fruit a capsule. NOTES: Tough drought-hardy plants that grow on rock platforms. Two spp. shed leaves in drought, others have resurrection capabilities, with 'apparently dead' plants, their leaves turned brown/orange, able to re-green and renew photosynthesis.

Dormant *Borya* plant.

Bulbine (Asphodelaceae): c.73 spp., most in tropical and South Africa, 6 spp. endemic in Aust. Annual or perennial, evergreen or resprouting, clumping/tufting lilies with fleshy roots and fleshy grass-like leaves, some also with a corm-like tuber. Racemes terminal on fleshy scapes. Flowers bisexual, usually yellow or orange, short-lived (hours). Tepals 6, equal. Stamens 6, filaments with prominent brush of hairs. Fruit a capsule. NOTES: Roots and tubers reportedly edible; leaves not edible but sap useful for treating insect bites and burns.

Calectasia (Dasypogonaceae): 15 spp., most endemic in WA. Perennial subshrubs with rhizomes or stilted sand-binding roots. Leaves sessile, basal sheaths persistent on stems. Flowers solitary, sessile, starry, often shiny, opening widely, lasting days. Tepals 6, equal, fused in basal half with spreading lobes, stiffly textured, pointed, blue or purple. Stamens yellow, ageing red or brown. Fruit indehiscent.

Calostemma (Amaryllidaceae): 3 spp., endemic in Aust. Decorative native bulbs that grow in crowded, localised clonal clumps, often in flood-prone sites. Deciduous in dry times. Leaves narrow in a basal group, elongating after flowering. Flowers funnel-shaped, colourful, scented, in groups atop tall scapes. Tepals 6, equal, fused at base with free lobes. Basal parts of stamen filaments fused to form a corona in 2 spp. Fruit indehiscent, globose.

Cartonema (Commelinaceae): 11 spp., most endemic in Aust.; also Trangan Is., Indon. Annual or perennial herbs, some with tubers. Leaves in a spiral, glandular-hairy. Infl. few-flowered, complex geometry. Flowers bisexual, short-lived (hours). Sepals 3. Petals 3, larger than sepals, flimsy, mostly yellow. Stamens 6. Fruit a capsule. NOTES: Distinctive lily-relatives from the tropics.

Chamaexeros (Asparagaceae): 4 spp., endemic in WA. Perennial, clumping herbs with short rhizomes and wiry roots. Leaves sessile, crowded, margins dry, membranous, often torn. Panicles sparse or compact. Flowers bisexual, opening widely, cream or yellow. Tepals 6, subsimilar, free. Fruit a capsule.

Commelina (Commelinaceae): 170 spp., 4 spp. in Aust. Prostrate annual or perennial herbs with erect to spreading fleshy stems and alternate leaves. Flowers grouped in leaf-like spathes, bisexual or male, short-lasting (hours). Sepals 3, shorter than petals. Petals 3, flimsy, one petal often much smaller than the others. Stamens 3, plus staminodes. Fruit a capsule. NOTES: Distinctive lily-relatives.

Conostylis (Haemodoraceae): 45 spp. endemic in WA. Tufted, clumping or spreading prostrate herbs with flat or terete leaves. Infl. 1- to many-flowered, often in a terminal cluster. Flowers bisexual, hairy. Perianth segments 6, fused basally, with erect/spreading lobes. Stamens 6. Fruit a capsule. NOTES: Important group of colourful lily-relatives common in the WA flora.

Crinum (Amaryllidaceae): 180 spp., 12 spp. in Aust, most endemic; also Africa, Asia. Either resprouting bulbous lilies or clumping perennials with an above ground pseudostem. Leaves deciduous or persistent, shiny. Flowers bisexual, in terminal clusters, each with a long slender tube and 6 spreading/recurving tepals. Stamens 6. Fruit indehiscent, globose. NOTES: Often forms spreading clonal colonies. Some spp. develop very large bulbs.

Curcuma (Zingiberaceae): 50 spp., 1 in Aust., not endemic; also NG, Asia. Resprouting herbs with tuberous rhizomes and leaves in a tuft. Infl. cylindrical, with fertile pouch-like bracts carrying the flowers and colourful sterile bracts topping the whole structure. Flowers tubular with free lobes, bisexual, white, pale green or yellow. Fruit a capsule.

Dasypogon (Dasypogonaceae): 3 spp., endemic in WA. Clumping perennials, occas. with a short trunk. Leaves narrow, flat or inrolled, roughened. Flowers small, not opening widely, crowded in globose heads atop sturdy scapes. Floral bracts sharply pointed. Sepals thick, fused above middle, hairy. Petals free, narrower than sepals. Fruit indehiscent.

Diplarrena (Iridaceae): 2 spp., endemic in Aust. Clumping, evergreen, perennial irids with rhizomes. Leaves flat, in fans. Infl. a small cluster of flowers enclosed in paired spathes, atop a long scape. Flowers zygomorphic, bisexual. Sepals 3, unequal. Petals 3, smaller than sepals, 2 spreading, 1 hooding stamens. Stamens 2. Fruit a capsule.

Doryanthes (Doryanthaceae): 2 spp., endemic in Aust. Large clumping plants. Leaves numerous, large, sword-shaped, flat, each with a brown tubular tip. Infl. a large compound raceme. Flowers bisexual, tubular at base with spreading lobes. Fruit a large capsule. NOTES: Distinctive frequently cultivated lily-relatives with spectacular nectar-rich flowers that attract birds.

Drymophila (Alstroemeriaceae): 2 spp., endemic in Aust. Perennials with thin wiry rhizomes and erect/arching leafy stems. Leaves alternate along stems, simple, shortly petiolate, spreading, midrib prominent. Flowers pendulous, arising singly or small groups in leaf axils. Tepals 6, subequal. Stamens 6. Fruit a spongy berry.

Eustrephus (Asparagaceae): Monotypic genus occurring in Aust., NG and Pacific Is.

Geitonoplesium (Asphodelaceae): Monotypic genus occurring in Aust., NG and Pacific Is.

Haemodorum (Haemodoraceae): 30 spp., most endemic in Aust., 1 NG. Either perennial herbs or resprouters. Rootstock orange/red. Leaves terete or flat, sheathing basally. Infl. a raceme or panicle. Flowers not opening widely. Tepals 6 in 2 equal or unequal whorls. Stamens 3. Fruit a capsule.

Helmholtzia (Phylidraceae): 3 spp., 2 endemic in Aust., 1 NG. Clumping lily-relatives. Leaves flat, sword-shaped, in fans. Panicles multi-flowered. Flowers bisexual, white or pink. Sepals 2, recurved, margins inrolled forming a hood. Petals 2, smaller than sepals. Stamen 1. Fruit either a capsule or indehiscent.

Herpolirion (Asphodelaceae): Monotypic genus occurring in Aust. and NZ.

Hypoxis (Hypoxidaceae): 110 spp., most in South Africa, 6 spp. endemic in Aust. Resprouters with fleshy corms (some exotics are evergreen). Most parts with silky hairs. Leaves basal, long, narrow. Infl. single-flowered or an umbel-like raceme. Flowers bisexual, starry, yellow. Petals shorter than sepals. Fruit a narrow capsule. NOTES: Roots are reportedly edible raw. See also *Pauridia*.

Isophysis (Iridaceae): Monotypic genus endemic in Tas.

Johnsonia (Asphodelaceae): 5 spp. endemic in WA. Perennial clumping/tufting herbs with narrow grass-like leaves, sheathing basally. Spikes terminal on thin scapes, each spike consisting of large overlapping dry bracts, lower 2 bracts empty, others enclose tiny bisexual flowers. Tepals 6, equal, fused at base, withering after flowering. Stamens 3, filaments broad. Fruit a capsule.

Kingia (Dasypogonaceae): Monotypic genus endemic in WA.

Lazarum (Araceae): 25 spp., many others unnamed, most Aust.; 1 NG. Deciduous, resprouting aroids with corms or rhizomes. Leaves 1-several, basal, petiolate; blades entire to deeply lobed. Infl. *Arum*-like, mostly solitary, often smelly, arising with or after leaves. Spathe flag-like, often black/purple. Flowers unisexual, tiny, on a fleshy spadix with separate male and female zones. Fruit a berry, often in clusters. Previously included in *Typhonium* (see also *Typhonium*).

Libertia (Iridaceae): 12 spp., 2 endemic in Aust.; NG, NZ, South America. Clumping, evergreen perennial irids. Leaves flat. Infl. a slender panicle. Flowers bisexual, opening widely, white, short-lived (hours). Petals similar size to sepals or larger. Stamens 3. Fruit a capsule.

Lomandra (Asparagaceae): 51 spp., many others unnamed, most endemic in Aust.; 2 in NG and NCal. Perennial, clumping, dioecious herbs. Leaves alternate in 2 opposite rows, apex occas. toothed. Male and female infl. similar or dissimilar. Flowers unisexual, separate or clustered; female flowers usually larger than males. Sepals and petals free or fused. Fruit a capsule. NOTES: Widespread important native group.

Macropidia (Haemodoraceae): Monotypic genus endemic in WA.

Molineria (Hypoxidaceae): 7 spp., 1 Asian sp. extending to n. Aust. Evergreen clumping lilies spreading by stolons. Leaves in a basal group, petiolate with a flat or ribbed blade. Infl. a compound multi-flowered head. Flowers bisexual, starry, yellow. Fruit a fleshy berry.

Murdannia (Commelinaceae): 50 spp., 4 spp. in Aust. Annual or perennial herbs, some with tuberous roots. Leaves in basal cluster, narrow. Infl. a panicle. Flowers bisexual, short-lived (hours). Sepals 3. Petals 3, flimsy, larger than sepals. Stamens 3, plus staminodes. Fruit a capsule. NOTES: Roots are reportedly edible raw.

Neoastelia (Asteliaceae): Monotypic genus endemic in NSW.

Orthrosanthus (Iridaceae): 9 spp., 4 endemic in Aust.; Mexico and America. Clumping, evergreen, perennial irids. Leaves flat, occas. rigid. Flowers bisexual, opening widely, blue, short-lived (hours). Tepals 6, subsimilar, spreading, fused at base. Stamens 3, free or base fused. Fruit a narrow capsule.

Patersonia (Iridaceae): 19 spp., 17 endemic in Aust.; NG, Indon. Clumping, evergreen perennial irids with a woody rhizome. Leaves flat, in fans. Flowers short-lived (hours), arising sporadically from a pair of leathery bracts, bisexual, opening widely, usually blue/violet. Sepals much larger than petals. Stamens 3, fused at base. Fruit a capsule.

Pauridia (Hypoxidaceae): 35 spp., most in South Africa, 5 spp. endemic in Aust. Resprouting glabrous lily-relatives with fleshy corms Leaves in a basal group, long, narrow. Infl. single-flowered or an umbel-like raceme. Flowers bisexual, starry, yellow. Tepals subsimilar, petals shorter than sepals. Fruit a narrow capsule. NOTES: Previously included in *Hypoxis*.

Phlebocarya (Haemodoraceae): 3 spp. endemic in WA. Perennial tufted or clumping herbs. Leaves basal, narrow, flat or terete, margins hairy. Infl. a panicle. Flowers starry, bisexual, white/cream. Perianth segments 6. Sepals and petals similar. Stamens 6. Fruit nut-like.

Pontederia (Pontederiaceae): 6 spp., 4 in Aust., 2 endemic. Aquatic herbs spreading by rhizomes. Leaves with sheathing base, swollen petiole and expanded blade. Flowers lily-like, bisexual, colourful, in axillary spikes or racemes, blue, purple or white. Tepals 6, similar. Fruit a capsule.

Proiphys (Amaryllidaceae): 5 spp. endemic in Aust. Resprouting bulbous lilies. Leaves expanding after flowering, basal, with long narrow petiole and wide blade. Flowers in terminal clusters, bisexual, funnel-shaped, scented. Tepals 6, fused at base. Stamens 6, at throat of perianth tube. Corona present. Fruit subglobose bulbils. NOTES: Attractive native bulbs that often form dense clonal patches.

Ripogonum (Ripogonaceae): 6 spp., 5 in Aust., 4 endemic. Climbers with smooth or prickly stems. Leaves alternate or opposite. Flowers bisexual, in axillary spikes or racemes, white, pale green or yellow. Tepals 6, similar. Fruit a berry.

Romnalda (Asparagaceae): 4 spp., 3 endemic in Qld; 1 in NG. Rainforest plants with stilt roots and narrow strap-like leaves in 2 spiral rows. Flowers small, bisexual, in clusters on panicle branches. Sepals 3, fused at base. Petals 3. Stamens 6. Fruit a capsule.

Sowerbaea (Asparagaceae): 5 spp. endemic in Aust. Perennial tufted lilies with narrow, terete or subterete leaves. Infl. a terminal mop-like umbel of crowded flowers atop a long scape. Flowers bisexual, spreading, drooping when finished. Tepals 6, subequal. Stamens 3, occas. also 3 staminodes. Fruit a capsule.

Thysanotus (Asparagaceae): 45 spp. in Aust., many others unnamed; also NG, Asia. Annual, perennial or resprouting (occas. evergreen), clumping/tufting or climbing lilies with fibrous or fleshy roots. Leaves mostly annual, often short-lived, narrow, green. Infl. raceme/panicle. Flowers bisexual, short-lived (hours), usually mauve/purple/pink. Sepals narrow. Petals much broader, margins conspicuously fringed. Fruit a capsule. NOTES: Roots of many spp. are reportedly edible raw.

Tribonanthes (Haemodoraceae): 10 spp. endemic in WA. Resprouting tuberous herbs. Leaves 1–4, basal and on stems, terete, hollow, base sheathing. Infl. terminal on scape, 1- to few-flowered. Flowers bisexual, woolly. Tepals 6, base fused and tubular, apex with erect/spreading/reflexed lobes. Stamens 6. Fruit a capsule.

Tripladenia (Colchicaceae): Monotypic genus endemic in Qld and NSW.

Typhonium (Araceae): 30 spp., most Asia, 2–3 in Aust. Deciduous, resprouting aroids with corms or rhizomes. Leaves basal, petiolate; blades entire to lobed. Infl. *Arum*-like, mostly solitary, arising after leaves. Spathe flag-like. Flowers unisexual, tiny, on a fleshy spadix with separate male and female zones. Fruit a berry. NOTES: See also *Lazarum*.

Wurmbea (Colchicaceae): 22 named spp. in Aust., many others unnamed; also Africa. Resprouting cormous herbs. Plants single or clumping. Leaves 2–3, base sheathing, often expanded, blade narrow, green. Flowers lasting several days, monoecious or dioecious. Tepals usually 6, narrow, with nectaries. Fruit a capsule. NOTES: Plants contain colchicine, a toxic alkaloid.

Xanthorrhoea (Asphodelaceae): 28 named spp. all endemic in Aust. Perennial tree-like or clumping plants with contractile roots, some have trunks covered with packed leaf bases. Leaves narrow in a green crown, old leaves in a grey/brown basal skirt. Infl. a long cylindrical spike on a woody base (scape). Flowers small, cream/white, bisexual, crowded, surrounded by packed bracts. Sepals and petals subsimilar, free. Fruit a woody capsule. NOTES: Best flowering after fire.

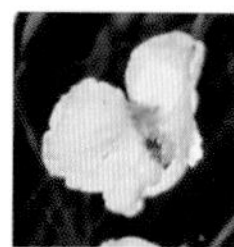

Xyris (Xyridaceae): 400 spp., 20 in Aust., most endemic; also many other countries. Annual or perennial herbs with fleshy rhizomes. Leaves basal, narrow, base open, sheathing. Infl. on rigid leafless stem, dense spikes with numerous bracts. Flowers 1 per bract, usually yellow, short lasting (hours). Sepals 3, narrow. Petals 3, flimsy, large. Fruit a capsule.

THE LILIES, THEIR RELATIVES AND LOOKALIKES

Orthrosanthus laxus.

TURQUOISE BERRY *Drymophila cyanocarpa*

SIZE/ID: Stems to 40cm long, branched or unbranched. Leaves to 8cm x 15mm, dark green, greyish beneath, veins prominent. Flowers 10–15mm across, white to pale mauve. Berries 5–10mm long, purplish blue, shiny. NOTES: Flowers last a few days, fruit hang longer unless eaten by birds. FLOWERING: Nov–Jan. RANGE/HABITAT: NSW (s from Braidwood), ACT, Vic, Tas. Coast to mountains in wetter forests, especially rainforest.

ORANGE BERRY *Drymophila moorei*

Fruit.

SIZE/ID: Stems to 30cm long, unbranched. Leaves to 6cm x 10–20mm, dark green, paler beneath, veins prominent. Flowers 10–15mm across, white to pale pink. Berries 8–15mm long, orange/yellow. FLOWERING: Oct–Jan.
RANGE/HABITAT: Qld (se), NSW (ne). Sheltered slopes and flats in wetter forests in mountains, especially rainforest.

EVERARD RANGE LILY *Calostemma abdicatum*

SIZE/ID: Leaves produced after flowers, to 70cm x 18mm, grey/green or glaucous. Infl. to 75cm tall, bearing 12–25 flowers in a 1-sided umbel. Flowers pendulous, 20–35mm long, basal tube pale, tepals pink/red, fragrant. NOTES: Rarely seen sp. Scapes carrying erect fruit elongate after flowering then topple to disperse mature fruit. FLOWERING: Mar–May.

RANGE/HABITAT: SA (Everard Ra.). Ephemeral stream beds and shady soil pockets on rocky slopes, gorges and gullies in sparse arid vegetation.

YELLOW GARLAND LILY *Calostemma luteum*

SIZE/ID: Leaves to 60cm x 10mm, dark green, shiny. Infl. to 50cm tall. Flowers 20–30 per umbel, spreading, 20–30mm long, yellow, often a few pink/red spots or lines at base, scented. NOTES: Has larger flowers with lobes more widely spreading than in *C. purpureum*. Multicoloured hybrids with *C. purpureum* are common in some areas. FLOWERING: Feb–Mar. RANGE/HABITAT: Qld (s), NSW (n), Vic (Merbein), SA (Lake Eyre basin). Floodplains in woodland and shrubland.

GARLAND LILY *Calostemma purpureum*

Pink variant.

SIZE/ID: Leaves to 60cm x 15mm, dark green, shiny. Infl. to 45cm tall. Flowers 12–25 per umbel, in a spreading group, 15–25mm long, pink/purple, sometime with a yellow throat, rarely very pale pink/white, strongly scented. NOTES: Often forms densely crowded clumps or spreading patches. Mixed colour hybrids with *C. luteum* are common in some areas. FLOWERING: Feb–Mar. RANGE/HABITAT: Inland parts of NSW, Vic, SA. Sparse forest, woodland and shrubland; often on flats near streams.

FLOODPLAIN LILY *Crinum arenarium*

SIZE/ID: Leaves to 100m x 6cm, erect to flaccid, bright green, shiny. Infl. to 1m tall. Flowers 6–14 per umbel, 10–20cm across, white/cream, scented. Perianth tube 8–13cm long. Tepals spreading or decurved, 10–15mm wide. Stamens all equal, to 6cm long, maroon. NOTES: Previously known as *C. angustifolium*. FLOWERING: Nov–Feb.
RANGE/HABITAT: NSW (n), WA (n), NT (n). Coastal and near-coastal floodplains and wet swampy sites.

DARLING LILY *Crinum flaccidum*

SIZE/ID: Leaves to 80cm x 5cm, erect, arching or flaccid, bright green, shiny. Infl. to 75cm tall. Flowers 8–16 per umbel, 10–20cm across, white/cream, strongly scented. Perianth tube 4–8cm long. Tepals spreading widely, 1–2cm wide. Stamens all equal, to 5.5cm long. NOTES: Widespread, common. Often in extensive patches. FLOWERING: Oct–Mar.

RANGE/HABITAT: Qld, NT, NSW, Vic (nw), SA (e), WA (nw), NT. Floodplains of inland rivers; beds of ephemeral streams.

YELLOW LILY *Crinum luteolum*

SIZE/ID: Leaves to 80cm x 5cm, erect to arching, bright green, shiny. Infl. to 75cm tall. Flowers 6–12 per umbel, 5–10cm across, light yellow, scented. Perianth tube 4–8cm long. Tepals spreading widely, 1–2cm wide. Lower 3 stamens shorter and closer together, upper 3 stamens longer and spread apart. NOTES: Often in extensive colonies. FLOWERING: Aug–Oct.
RANGE/HABITAT: SA (Flinders Ra.). Rocky hills in well-drained soil.

SWAMP LILY, MANGROVE LILY *Crinum pedunculatum*

SIZE/ID: Perennial clumper 1–2m tall with thick pseudostems to 45cm long. Leaves to 1.5m x 15cm, dark green, erect to spreading. Infl. to 1.5m tall. Flowers 20–40 per umbel, 10–20cm across, white, scented. Perianth tube to 9.5cm long. Tepals spreading or decurved, 9–10mm wide. NOTES: Impressive sp. FLOWERING: Nov–Feb. RANGE/HABITAT: Qld (n to s), NSW (s to Durras), NT (n, islands); also NG, NCal. Estuaries, stream banks and coastal swamps.

LOWLAND BUSH LILY *Crinum uniflorum*

SIZE/ID: Leaves few, to 40cm x 2mm, erect to arching, bright green, shiny. Infl. to 80cm tall. Flower single (occas. 2), sessile, 10–20cm across, white, occas. pinkish, lightly scented. Perianth tube 7–13cm long. Tepals spreading to decurved, 5–12mm wide. Stamens all equal, pink/purple. NOTES: Distinctive for its 1–2 flowers. Often in spreading patches. FLOWERING: Nov–Mar.
RANGE/HABITAT: Qld (n), NT (n). Seasonally inundated sandy flats.

BUSH LILY *Crinum venosum*

SIZE/ID: Leaves to 40cm x 4cm, erect, arching or flaccid, bright green, shiny. Infl. to 80cm tall. Flowers sessile, 5–8 per umbel, 10–20cm across, white/cream, scented. Perianth tube 5–12cm long. Tepals spreading or decurved, 7–17mm wide. Stamens all equal, short, pink. FLOWERING: Nov–Feb.
RANGE/HABITAT: Qld (Torres Strait Is., Cape York Pen.), NT (Arnhem Land). Near-coastal to hinterland forest and woodland.

SPOON LILY *Proiphys alba*

SIZE/ID: Leaves to 70cm long, light green to grey/green; blades to 35 x 10cm, elliptical, base tapered, apex pointed. Infl. to 60cm tall. Flowers 10–30 per umbel, 15–25mm across, bell-shaped, white with yellow anthers, crowded, spreading or pendulous, fragrant. Perianth tube to 15mm long. Corona 5–12mm long. FLOWERING: Dec–Mar.

RANGE/HABITAT: Qld (n, islands), NT (n, islands); also NG. Seasonally wet areas in paperbark woodland.

CHRISTMAS LILY *Proiphys amboinensis*

SIZE/ID: Leaves to 1m long, bright green shiny; blades to 35 x 35cm, nearly circular, base incurved. Infl. to 90cm tall. Flowers 5–25 per umbel, 45–55mm across, broadly bell-shaped or nearly flat, erect to spreading, white with yellow throat and anthers, fragrant. Perianth tube to 35mm long. Corona 7–10mm long. NOTES: Often forms huge spreading colonies. FLOWERING: Nov–Mar. RANGE/HABITAT: Qld (Torres Strait Is. to Cardwell); also NG, Pacific Is. Flats and slopes in rainforest, monsoon thickets and other wetter forests.

BRISBANE LILY *Proiphys cunninghamii*

SIZE/ID: Leaves to 60cm long, bright green, shiny; blades to 25 x 13cm, ovate, bright green, base rounded. Infl. to 80cm tall. Flowers 5–12 per umbel, 15–30mm across, nearly flat or with recurved tips, spreading or pendulous, white with yellow anthers, fragrant. Perianth tube to 12mm long. Corona 12–20mm long. FLOWERING: Dec–May.

RANGE/HABITAT: Qld (se), NSW (ne). Flats and gullies on rainforest margins and in other wetter forests, occas. among rocks.

TOWNSVILLE LILY *Proiphys infundibularis*

SIZE/ID: Leaves to 80cm long, bright green shiny; blades to 30 x 28cm, ovate/elliptic, margins often wavy, base incurved. Infl. to 90cm tall. Flowers 5–16 per umbel, 35–45mm across, funnel-shaped, on short thickish pedicels, erect to suberect, white with cream/yellow anthers, fragrant. Perianth tube to 25mm long. Corona 14–16mm long. FLOWERING: Nov–May.
RANGE/HABITAT: Qld (Townsville to Conway Ra.). Open forest and deciduous vine thickets, often among boulders.

KIMBERLEY LILY *Proiphys kimberleyensis*

SIZE/ID: Leaves to 50cm long, leathery, green/glaucous; blades to 27 x 14cm, elliptical/ovate, base tapered. Flower stems to 65cm tall. Flowers 17–21 per umbel, 25–45mm across, broadly funnel-shaped, on long thin pedicels, erect to suberect, white with yellow anthers, fragrant. Perianth tube to 23mm long. Corona flattish, yellow centre. NOTES: Flowers appear before the leaves. Rare sp. in small, localised patches. FLOWERING: Dec–Feb. RANGE/HABITAT: WA (Kimberley region). Shallow red clay over basalt in woodland.

SWEET SNAKESKIN LILY *Amorphophallus galbra*

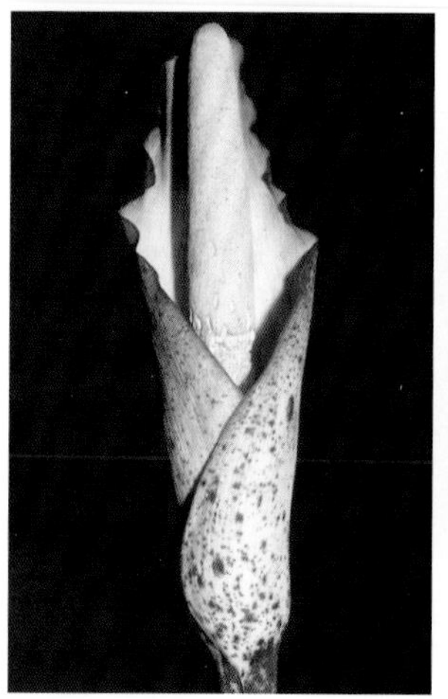

Fruit.

SIZE/ID: Plants to 1m tall. Petiole smooth, mottled. Leaf blades 2–3 times forked, pale green, tips pointed. Scape to 80cm tall. Spathe erect, 10–36cm long, greyish, speckled/mottled with a wide range of colours. Spadix equal to or shorter than spathe, finger-like, whitish. Berries red. NOTES: Forms clonal colonies. Flowers with sweet or fruity smell. FLOWERING: Dec–Feb.
RANGE/HABITAT: Tropical n Qld, NT, WA; also NG. Monsoon forests, vine thickets, rainforest.

ELEPHANT FOOT LILY *Amorphophallus paeoniifolius*

SIZE/ID: Leaf to 2m tall. Petiole strongly warty, mottled grey/green. Leaf blades forking freely, pale green, tips pointed. Scape to 80cm tall. Spathe spreading, 30–40cm long and wide, reddish/purple, mottled. Spadix shorter than spathe, whitish, with inflated purple appendix. Berries red. NOTES: Forms clonal colonies. Flowers with smell of rotting flesh. Grown for its edible tubers. FLOWERING: Oct–Nov.

RANGE/HABITAT: Qld (Torres Strait Is.), NT (n); also Madagascar, Asia, Oceania. Monsoon forests.

BLACK ARUM LILY *Lazarum brownii*

SIZE/ID: Rhizomes to 15 x 3cm. Leaves several. Petioles 10–70cm long. Blades deeply divided into grey/green lobes. Scape short. Spathe to 20 x 12cm, concave, deep purple/brown internally, green externally, tip attenuate. Spadix shorter than spathe, dark purple/brown. NOTES: Forms clonal colonies, spreading by rhizomes and bulbils. Flowers smell like rotting meat. FLOWERING: Dec–Feb. RANGE/HABITAT: Qld, NSW (Rockhampton to Menangle). Wetter forests, gullies, stream banks.

TIWI LILY *Lazarum jonesii*

SIZE/ID: Rhizomes cormous. Leaves 3–6, erect/arching. Petioles 5–13cm long. Blades deeply 3-lobed, the pale green lobes narrow to broad (10–35mm wide). Infl. among leaf bases. Spathe to 10 x 4cm, deep reddish-purple inside, greenish brown to reddish outside, apex pointed. Spadix shorter than spathe, dark red. NOTES: Rare sp. that grows in small patches, spreading by stolons. FLOWERING: Dec. RANGE/HABITAT: NT (Bathurst Is., Melville Is.). Among litter in moist forest.

KIMBERLEY ARUM LILY *Lazarum liliifolium*

SIZE/ID: Rhizomes cormous. Leaves 5–8, to 60cm long, erect, strap-like, not lobed, grey/green, narrow, channelled. Infl. among leaf bases. Spathe to 25 x 10cm, reddish-brown inside, green to brownish outside, apex pointed. Spadix shorter than spathe, red with white band of male flowers. NOTES: Grows in crowded clonal clumps. Leaves and flowers emerge together. FLOWERING: Nov–Feb.

RANGE/HABITAT: WA (Kimberley), NT (Victoria R.). Woodland.

BROWN ARUM LILY *Lazarum wilbertii*

SIZE/ID: Rhizomes cormous, to 4cm diam. Leaves 4–6. Petioles 15–50cm long. Blades triangular, bluish to grey/green. Infl. among leaves. Spathe to 33 x 13cm, concave, deep purple internally, green/brown externally, tip pointed. Spadix shorter than spathe, dark purple/black. Berries orange. NOTES: Forms small clonal clumps. Flowers smell like rotting meat. FLOWERING: Jan–Feb. RANGE/HABITAT: Qld (Cape York to Palm Cove). Among litter in moist forest.

WHIPTAIL LILY *Typhonium flagelliforme*

SIZE/ID: Rhizomes cormous. Leaves 2–3, prostrate. Petioles 10–30cm long. Blades entire, to 25 x 10cm, pale green with paler veins. Infl. among leaf bases. Spathe to 25 x 3cm, greenish or whitish, attenuated, apex drawn into long point, recurved or coiled. Spadix as long as spathe, yellowish, drawn into long thin point. NOTES: Forms small clonal groups, spreading by stolons. Medicinally important. FLOWERING: Nov–Jan. RANGE/HABITAT: Qld (n), NT (n); also NG, Indonesia, Asia. Wetter forests.

PURPLE CHOCOLATE LILY *Arthropodium capillipes*

SIZE/ID: Leaves 5–15, to 30cm x 7.5mm, green. Panicles to 1.5m tall. Pedicels 1–2cm long. Flowers 2–4 per axil, 15–22mm across, nodding, dark purple to pink, fragrant. Sepals to 3mm wide. Petals to 5mm wide. Anthers purple with densely hairy, dark purple appendages. Filaments bent sharply near apex. NOTES: PKA *Dichopogon capillipes*. FLOWERING: Sep–Jan.
RANGE/HABITAT: WA (Perth to Cape Naturaliste). Drier open forest and woodland.

PALE VANILLA LILY *Arthropodium curvipes*

SIZE/ID: Leaves 4–10, to 10cm x 10mm (occas. very short and narrow), usually withered. Infl. to 25cm tall, unbranched or 1-branched. Pedicels to 13mm long, decurved. Flowers 1 per axil, 8–10mm across, nodding, pinkish, mauve or whitish. Tepals to 3mm wide. Filament hairs mostly cream/white, purple group near anther.
FLOWERING: Aug–Sep.
RANGE/HABITAT: WA (Coolgardie to Merredin). Granite outcrops, often under shrubs.

NODDING CHOCOLATE LILY *Arthropodium fimbriatum*

SIZE/ID: Leaves 5–15, to 35cm x 3mm, usually withered. Infl. to 80cm tall, erect/arching, unbranched or 1–2 branches. Pedicels to 15mm long, erect. Flowers several per axil, nodding, 10–25mm across, mauve/purple, chocolate-scented. Sepals to 4mm wide. Petals to 6mm wide, finely fringed. Anthers purple with densely hairy purple appendages. NOTES: PKA *Dichopogon fimbriatus.* Common sp., occas. grows in extensive patches. FLOWERING: Sep–Feb.
RANGE/HABITAT: NSW, Vic, SA, WA. Drier forests and woodland.

PALE VANILLA LILY *Arthropodium milleflorum*

SIZE/ID: Leaves 1–17, to 60cm x 17mm, pale green. Infl. to 1m tall, sparsely branched or unbranched. Pedicels to 15mm long. Flowers 2–9 per axil, 10–15mm across, white to pinkish/blue, fragrant. Sepals to 3.5mm wide. Petals to 6mm wide. Filament hairs mostly cream/white, purple group near anther. NOTES: Common sp.
FLOWERING: Sep–Mar.
RANGE/HABITAT: Qld (se), NSW, Vic, Tas, SA (se). Moist areas in open forest, grassy forest and grassland.

SMALL VANILLA LILY *Arthropodium minus*

SIZE/ID: Leaves 1–14, to 30cm x 5mm, often withered. Infl. to 50cm tall, usually unbranched, occas. sparsely branched. Pedicels to 20mm long. Flowers 1–2 per axil, nodding, 6–10mm across, deep pink, mauve or white, fragrant. Sepals to 3.5mm wide. Petals to 5mm wide. Filament hairs white to purple. FLOWERING: Aug–Dec. RANGE/HABITAT: Qld (se), NSW, Vic, Tas, SA. Drier forest, grassland, moss cushions over rock plates.

DROOPING VANILLA LILY *Arthropodium pendulum*

SIZE/ID: Leaves 1–17, to 30cm x 8mm. Infl. to 50cm tall, usually unbranched. Pedicels to 10mm long. Flowers 1–2 per axil, nodding, 8–16mm across, mauve/pink, strongly fragrant. Sepals to 3.5mm wide. Petals to 6mm wide, margins irregular. Filament hairs white in basal two-thirds, dark purple near anther. FLOWERING: Sep–Dec. RANGE/HABITAT: Tas. Montane to alpine localities; moist/damp areas on slopes in grassland and grassy forests.

CHOCOLATE LILY *Arthropodium strictum*

SIZE/ID: Leaves 5–15, to 60cm x 10mm, dark green, flat. Infl. to 1.2m tall, erect, usually branched. Pedicels to 35mm long, erect. Flowers 1 per axil, more or less erect, 15–25mm across, mauve/purple, chocolate-scented. Sepals to 4mm wide. Petals to 8mm wide. Anthers purple with bright yellow appendages. NOTES: PKA *Dichopogon strictus*. Common sp., occas. grows in extensive patches. Roots are reportedly edible raw. FLOWERING: Oct–Jan. RANGE/HABITAT: NSW, Vic, Tas, SA (se). Drier forests, grassy forest, grassland, rocky hills.

NATIVE ASPARAGUS *Asparagus racemosus*

SIZE/ID: Roots tuberous. Climber to 4m tall, often in tangled masses. Cladodes 3–6 per axil, to 30 x 1mm, green, with spines to 4mm long. Racemes to 10cm long. Flowers 4–6mm across, white, often in pairs. Tepals narrow, spreading. Anthers orange. Berry 5–6mm across, globose, red. NOTES: Birds eat the fruit. Medicinal plant. Roots and young shoots are edible. AKA *Protasparagus racemosus*. FLOWERING: Aug–Jan.
RANGE/HABITAT: Tropical Qld, NT, WA. Watercourses in woodland.

LITTLE FRINGE-LEAF *Chamaexeros serra*

SIZE/ID: Clumping plant with short, knotted rhizomes covered with persistent old leaves. Roots thin, wiry. Leaves crowded, to 20cm x 4mm, flat, green, margins papery, whitish, lacerated. Panicles short, to 10cm long, compact. Flowers clustered in leaf bases, 8–12mm across, yellow, anthers protruding, yellow. Capsules 5–6mm long.
FLOWERING: Aug–Nov.
RANGE/HABITAT: WA (Dongara to Ravensthorpe). Forests, shrubland and granite outcrops in sand, gravel or laterite.

WOMBAT BERRY *Eustrephus latifolius*

Fruit.

SIZE/ID: Monotypic genus in Aust., NG, Pacific Is. Climber with tough, wiry stems to 10m tall. Leaves to 12cm x 35mm, dark green, paler beneath. Flowers in upper axils, 10–18mm across, pink to mauve, ageing white. Petals fringed with long hairs. Capsules 10–20mm across, yellow/orange. Seeds black with edible aril.
NOTES: Exhibits much variation in leaf size. Roots are edible raw.
FLOWERING: Aug–Mar.
RANGE/HABITAT: Qld (n to Cape York), NSW, Vic. Forest, heath and rainforest margins.

COCKY'S BOOTLACE *Lomandra banksii*

SIZE/ID: Stems to 3m tall, unbranched or few branches. Leaves to 45cm x 10mm, spreading to recurved, tough, green, apex toothed. Male and female panicles similar, longer than leaves. Flowers c.2.5mm across, in separate tight clusters, bell-shaped, white. Petals 3–4mm long. Capsules 10mm long, brownish, opening star-like to expose seeds covered in bright red aril. FLOWERING: Sep–Mar.
RANGE/HABITAT: Qld (Cape York to Cardwell); also NG, NCal. Coastal forests and shrubland in sand; rainforest margins.

SCENTED MAT-RUSH *Lomandra effusa*

Male flowers.

SIZE/ID: Plants to 60cm wide. Leaves to 50cm x 1.3mm, spreading, stiff, blue/green. Female infl. smaller than male, both much-branched. Flowers funnel-shaped or starry, white, mauve or pink, strongly scented. Petals to 6mm long. Male flowers with narrower segments than females. NOTES: Widespread in drier inland areas FLOWERING: Sporadic after rain.
RANGE/HABITAT: NSW, Vic (nw.), SA, WA. Shrubland on plains, clay pans and rock outcrops.

WOOLLY MAT-RUSH *Lomandra leucocephala*

Subsp. *robusta.*

Subsp. *leucocephala.*

SIZE/ID: Plants to 60cm tall. Leaves to 60cm x 2mm, rigid, grey/green, veins prominent. Male and female flowers similar, crowded in spherical head-like clusters, cream/white, sweetly scented. Subsp. *robusta* from northern and inland areas grows larger than subsp. *leucocephala*, has broader leaves (to 5mm wide) and male infl. with more than 3 heads of flowers. NOTES: Widespread, common, especially inland. FLOWERING: Jul–Sep. RANGE/HABITAT: Qld, NSW, Vic, SA, NT, WA. Mallee scrub and heath on sandy slopes.

SPRAWLING MAT-RUSH *Lomandra obliqua*

Female flowers.

Male flowers.

SIZE/ID: Stems sprawling to scrambling, freely branching. Leaves to 8cm x 2mm, spreading, often twisted, green to bluish, apex pointed. Male spikes to 10cm long. Female infl. a globose head 5–8cm across. Flowers yellow with purple tints. Petals 2–3mm long. FLOWERING: Sep–Dec.
RANGE/HABITAT: Qld, NSW (Blackdown Tlnd to Jervis Bay). Coast to tlnds in forests in sand and among rocks.

STILT LILY *Romnalda grallata*

Buds and flowers.

SIZE/ID: Plants to 40cm tall. Stems breaking free of ground, supported by stilt roots. Leaves to 35cm x 15mm, spreading, often curved, bright green, occas. with transverse wrinkles. Panicles to 30cm tall, erect, branches wiry. Flowers in clusters, 6–8mm across, whitish with purple marks. Perianth base tubular. Tepals spreading or recurved. Capsules 1cm long. FLOWERING: Oct–Jan. RANGE/HABITAT: Qld (ne). Lowland to highland rainforest in granitic loam.

RUSH LILY *Sowerbaea juncea*

SIZE/ID: Leaves to 50cm x 2mm, terete, green, spreading. Infl. to 75cm tall, erect. Pedicels to 14mm long, spreading to decurved. Flowers 30–40 per umbel, crowded, each flower 10–16mm across, mauve, pink or white. Anthers yellow/orange. NOTES: Widespread and common. FLOWERING: Mainly Aug–Jan.
RANGE/HABITAT: Qld (N to Rockhampton), NSW, Vic, Tas (n). Coast/near-coastal heath to montane grass and heath, mainly in damp/moist soil.

PURPLE TASSELS *Sowerbaea laxiflora*

SIZE/ID: Leaves to 30cm x 1mm, flat, green, spreading. Infl. to 70cm tall, erect. Pedicels to 14mm long, spreading to decurved. Flowers 30–40 per umbel, crowded, each flower 10–15mm across, purple, pink or white. Anthers yellow/orange, conspicuous. NOTES: Occas. in large patches. FLOWERING: Aug–Nov.
RANGE/HABITAT: WA (Kalbarri to Denmark). Coast/near-coastal heath and woodland in sand and clay.

BANKS'S FRINGE LILY *Thysanotus banksii*

SIZE/ID: Clumping resprouter. Leaves 3–5, to 60cm x 1mm. Infl. annual, sparsely branched near apex, to 60cm tall. Flowers 1–2 per umbel, 15–20mm across, purple. Sepals shorter and narrower than petals. Petals to 10 x 8mm, including fringe to 3mm long. Stamens 6; anthers twisted, outer 3 to 3mm long, curved, purple, 3 inner to 4mm long, yellow. NOTES: Wrongly recorded from WA.
FLOWERING: Jan–Jul.
RANGE/HABITAT: Tropical Qld, NT; also NG. Grassy forest, paperbark wetland, wet heath.

MALLEE FRINGE LILY *Thysanotus baueri*

SIZE/ID: Clumping resprouter. Leaves 3–5, to 13 x 1mm, usually withered. Infl. annual, to 35cm tall, unbranched or branched. Flowers 1–4 per umbel, 15–25mm across, bluish/purple. Sepals c.2mm wide, margins often paler. Petals to 7mm wide, including fringe to 2mm long. Stamens 6; anthers curved, twisted, outer 3 to 4mm long, inner 3 to 7mm long. FLOWERING: Sep–Jan. RANGE/HABITAT: NSW (w), Vic (ne), SA (s), WA (se). Inland mallee, native pine forests and *Triodia*/grassy plains, often in sand.

LONG-LEAVED FRINGE LILY *Thysanotus elatior*

SIZE/ID: Clumping resprouter. Leaves 4–15, flat, to 55cm x 2.2mm. Panicles annual, to 85cm tall. Flowers 1–4 per umbel, 35–50mm across, pink to purple. Sepals c. 2.5mm wide. Petals to 20mm wide, including fringe to 6.5mm long. Stamens 6; anthers not twisted, outer 3 c.6mm long, yellow, inner 3 c.10mm long, curved, purple.
FLOWERING: Jan–May; also sporadic.
RANGE/HABITAT: Tropical NT (including islands), WA (n). Grassy forest, woodland and seasonally wet sites.

RUSH FRINGE LILY *Thysanotus juncifolius*

SIZE/ID: Clumping lily. Leaves 0–3, to 25cm x 1mm, nearly terete. Infl. perennial, to 60cm tall, forking, stems striate. Flowers 1–5 per umbel, 20–28mm across, mauve/purple. Sepals to 2mm wide. Petals to 9mm wide, including fringe to 4.5mm long. Stamens 6; anthers twisted, outer 3 to 4mm long, purple/yellow, straight, inner 3 to 9mm long, purple, curved. FLOWERING: Sep–Mar. RANGE/HABITAT: NSW (s), Vic (e), SA (se). Coast to ranges in forest and heath, occas. swampy.

MANGLES' FRINGE LILY *Thysanotus manglesianus*

SIZE/ID: Resprouting climber with annual stems. Leaves 1–2, to 20cm long. Stem 1, leafless, to 2m long, twining or prostrate, forking freely. Flowers 20–32mm across, mauve/purple. Sepals to 3mm wide. Petals to 8.5mm wide, including fringe to 2.5mm long. Stamens 6; anthers not twisted, purple, outer 3 to 4mm long, inner 3 to 6mm long, curved. FLOWERING: Aug–Nov.
RANGE/HABITAT: WA (Meekatharra to Balladonia). Forest, mallee and granite outcrops in sand and laterite.

FRILLY KNICKERS *Thysanotus multiflorus*

SIZE/ID: Clumping perennial lily. Leaves perennial, 3–30, to 90cm x 5mm. Infl. annual, single, to 70cm tall, with an apical umbel (occas. a secondary umbel below) containing 40–60 flowers. Flowers 15–35mm across. Sepals to 2.5mm wide. Petals to 13mm wide, including fringe to 5mm long. Stamens 3; anthers curved.
FLOWERING: Aug–Jan.
RANGE/HABITAT: WA (Avon Valley to Cape Riche). Coastal *Banksia* forest in white sand and jarrah forest in laterite.

TWINING FRINGE LILY *Thysanotus patersonii*

SIZE/ID: Resprouting climber with annual stems. Leaves annual, often absent, 1–2, to 20cm long, terete. Stems 1–2, leafless, to 1m long, forking, climbing by twining or prostrate. Flowers 15–20mm across, mauve/purple. Sepals to 4mm wide. Petals to 6mm wide, including fringe to 1mm long. Stamens 6; anthers not twisted, straight, equal length. NOTES: Variable sp. under study. FLOWERING: Aug–Nov.

RANGE/HABITAT: NSW, ACT, Vic, Tas, SA, WA. Coast to ranges in forest, shrubland and heath.

FEW-FLOWERED FRINGE LILY *Thysanotus pauciflorus*

SIZE/ID: Small clumping perennial lily. Leaves perennial, to 7cm x 3mm, flat. Infl. annual, single, to 1m long, erect or sprawling, with an apical few-flowered umbel. Flowers 18–22mm across. Sepals to 4mm wide. Petals to 11mm wide, including fringe to 3mm long. Stamens 3; anthers shallowly curved. FLOWERING: Sep–Jan. RANGE/HABITAT: WA (Stirling Ra. to Hopetoun). Coastal scrub and mallee in moist/wet peaty sand.

PYRAMIDAL FRINGE LILY *Thysanotus thyrsoideus*

SIZE/ID: Clumping resprouter. Leaves 1–5, to 60cm x 1mm, base often purple. Panicle pyramidal, to 65cm tall. Flowers 1–5 per umbel, 15–28mm across. Sepals to 2mm wide. Petals to 9mm wide, including fringe to 3mm long. Stamens 6; anthers twisted, outer 3 to 5mm long, inner 3 to 9mm long, curved. NOTES: Variable sp. under study. FLOWERING: Sep–Nov.
RANGE/HABITAT: WA (Gin Gin to Cape Riche). Coast to wheatbelt in forest and heath, occas. seasonally wet. (76)

COMMON FRINGE LILY *Thysanotus tuberosus*

SIZE/ID: Clumping resprouter. Leaves 5–15, to 60cm x 2mm, glaucous. Infl. annual, to 80cm tall, much branched. Flowers 1–8 per umbel, 15–35mm across, mauve/purple, occas. white. Sepals 1.5–2mm wide. Petals to 12mm wide, including fringe to 4mm long. Stamens 6; anthers twisted, 3 outer anthers to 4.5mm long, 3 inner to 9mm long. NOTES: Widespread, common. Roots are edible raw. Wrongly recorded from WA. FLOWERING: Aug–Apr. RANGE/HABITAT: Qld, NSW, ACT, Vic, SA. Coast to inland in forest and heath.

FALSE BLIND GRASS *Agrostocrinum scabrum*

SIZE/ID: Leaves to 40cm x 8mm. Panicle to 30 x 30cm. Pedicels to 30mm long, glabrous. Flowers 25–32mm across, dark blue. Tepals 6–8mm wide. Stamens 6mm long, black, twisted away from style. Capsules to 5mm wide, glabrous. NOTES: Plants killed by fire. Massed flowering of seedlings in years after fire. FLOWERING: Sep–Dec.

RANGE/HABITAT: WA (Watheroo to Cape Arid). Woodland, mallee, shrubland and heath.

COMMON BULBINE LILY *Bulbine bulbosa*

SIZE/ID: Perennial with thick roots, tuber vertical. Leaves to 50cm x 8mm, channelled, green, often slightly roughened. Racemes 20–50cm tall, stems terete. Flowers 20–40mm across, yellow. Stamens 6, equal, erect with bunched anthers and clubbed yellow/brown hairs. Capsules 4–7mm diam. NOTES: Complex variable sp. widely distributed from coast to mountains and plains. FLOWERING: Aug–Jan.

RANGE/HABITAT: Qld (se), NSW, Vic, SA (se), Tas. Grassland, forest, swamps and herbfields, in moist soil.

COASTAL BULBINE LILY *Bulbine crassa*

SIZE/ID: Robust perennial spreading by offsets. Leaves to 50cm x 30mm, erect, fleshy, channelled, grey/green. Racemes 1–2, 20–50cm tall, stems thick, fleshy. Flowers 20–25mm across, yellow. Stamens 6, unequal, 3 longer with dense hairs below anther, 3 shorter with few/no hairs. Capsules 5–7mm diam. FLOWERING: Sep–Feb.

RANGE/HABITAT: Vic (Wilsons Promontory, Cape Conron), Tas (eastern Bass Strait Is.). Coastal boulders subject to salt spray.

INLAND BULBINE LILY *Bulbine fraseri*

SIZE/ID: Perennial with fleshy roots, tuber horizontal. Leaves erect to flaccid, to 80cm x 14mm, channelled, green/glaucous, filled with clear mucous. Racemes 50–120cm tall, stems terete. Flowers 24–46mm across, yellow/orange. Stamens 6, 2 erect, 4 spreading, all with needle-like yellow/orange hairs. Capsules 5–8mm diam.
NOTES: Locally abundant in good seasons. FLOWERING: Spring/ summer after rain.
RANGE/HABITAT: Inland areas of Qld, NSW, SA. Dry grassland on cracking clay plains.

NATIVE LEEK *Bulbine glauca*

SIZE/ID: Perennial with thick roots, no tuber. Leaves to 30cm x 10mm, channelled, usually glaucous. Racemes 50–110cm tall, stems terete. Flowers 20–35mm across, yellow. Stamens 6, equal, loosely grouped, all with clubbed yellow hairs ending well below anthers. Capsules 4–6mm diam. NOTES: Tall, graceful lily.
FLOWERING: Aug–Jan.
RANGE/HABITAT: NSW (s from Bungonia, disjunct on New England Tlnd), Vic, Tas. Mainly rock outcrops and cliffs in mountains and wetter forests; to coastal areas in Tas.

ANNUAL NATIVE LEEK *Bulbine semibarbata*

SIZE/ID: Annual with fibrous roots, no tuber. Leaves to 20cm x 5mm, green. Racemes 10–30cm tall, stems terete. Flowers 6–15mm across, yellow. Stamens 6, 3 long with yellow hairs, 3 shorter with no hairs. Anthers red or brown. Capsules 2–4mm diam. NOTES: Complex variable sp. widely distributed from coast to inland plains. FLOWERING: Jul–Feb.

RANGE/HABITAT: Qld (s), NSW, Vic, Tas, SA, WA. Rocky outcrops, dunes, shrubland, margins of salt lakes and swamps.

CLIFFTOP BULBINE LILY *Bulbine vagans*

SIZE/ID: Perennial with fleshy roots, no tuber. Leaves numerous, crowded, to 30cm x 8mm, terete, shiny. Racemes straggly, 30–60cm tall, stems angular. Flowers 15–25mm across. Stamens 3 long, 3 shorter, closely bunched to one side, all with clubbed yellow or red hairs. Capsules 3–5mm long. NOTES: Grows in localised patches.
FLOWERING: Aug–Feb.
RANGE/HABITAT: Qld, NSW (Kroombit Tops to Dangars Falls). Crevices in rocky cliff tops and adjacent herbfield.

BLUE GRASS LILY *Caesia calliantha*

SIZE/ID: Leaves to 50cm x 15mm. Infl. 20–70cm tall, simple or branched. Flowers 1–3 per cluster, 15–22mm across, pale blue to purple with darker nerves. Stamens 3–5mm long. Anthers c. 1mm long, yellow. Filaments swollen, white with purple apical ring or wholly purple. Capsules 4–8mm wide. NOTES: Widespread and variable sp. FLOWERING: Sep–Jan.
RANGE/HABITAT: NSW (mainly s, disjunct on New England Tlnd), Vic, Tas, SA (s). Grassland and grassy forest.

WESTERN GRASS LILY *Caesia occidentalis*

SIZE/ID: Leaves to 60cm x 5mm, stiffly upright. Infl. 40–70cm tall, simple or branched. Flowers 1–3 per cluster, 10–20mm across, white, externally green/brown, with darker nerves. Stamens 4.5–5mm long. Anthers c. 1mm long, yellow. Filaments c. 4mm long, narrowly swollen, flattish, white/greenish or yellow. Capsules 5–8mm across. NOTES: Variable sp. under study. FLOWERING: Sep–Feb.
RANGE/HABITAT: WA (Jurien to Esperance). Wetter areas in forest, swamps and heath.

SMALL GRASS LILY *Caesia parviflora*

SIZE/ID: Leaves to 50cm x 5mm. Panicle 20–70cm tall. Flowers 2–6 per cluster, 10–15mm across, usually white, occas. bluish or pinkish, with darker nerves. Stamens 3–4.5mm long. Anthers c. 1mm long, yellow. Filaments c. 3mm long, narrowly swollen, white/greenish. Capsules 4–5mm across. FLOWERING: Sep–Apr. RANGE/HABITAT: Qld (n to Rockhampton), NSW, Vic, Tas, SA. Moisture-retentive soils in grassland, grassy forest and heath.

TROPICAL GRASS LILY *Caesia setifera*

SIZE/ID: Leaves to 50cm x 2mm. Infl. 30–60cm tall, simple or branched. Flowers 1–9 per cluster (usually 3), 12–20mm across, white to pale blue or purple, with darker blue nerves. Stamens 5–6mm long. Anthers c. 1mm long, yellow. Filaments c. 4.5mm long, narrowly swollen, base sharply bent/curved, golden yellow, apex blue/purple. Capsules 4–5mm across. FLOWERING: Dec–Apr. RANGE/HABITAT: Tropical parts of Qld, NT and WA; also NG. Grassy woodland, swamps and blacksoil plains.

BANDED GRASS LILY *Caesia vittata*

SIZE/ID: Leaves to 70cm x 8mm. Infl. 50–70cm tall, branched. Flowers 2–6 per cluster, 15–18mm across, pale blue, with darker blue nerves. Stamens 5–6mm long. Anthers c. 1mm long, yellow. Filaments c. 4.5mm long, base swollen, blue with white bands. Capsules 4–6mm wide. NOTES: AKA *Caesia parviflora* var. *vittata*.
FLOWERING: Sep–Apr.
RANGE/HABITAT: Qld (n to Bundaberg), NSW, Vic, Tas. Moist to wet soils in grassland and grassy forest.

BLUE SQUILL *Chamaescilla corymbosa*

SIZE/ID: Leaves 5–15 per shoot, spreading, flat, to 25cm x 6mm, dark green. Infl. to 40cm tall, branched, 1–15-flowered, each flower 12–20mm across, usually blue with darker nerves, occas. pinkish or white. NOTES: Carpets the ground with blue in some areas of WA.
FLOWERING: Jul–Jan.
RANGE/HABITAT: Vic, Tas, SA, WA. Banksia woodland, grassy forest and heath in moist sandy soil.

CLAYPAN SQUILL *Chamaescilla gibsonii*

SIZE/ID: Clumping lily. Leaves 15–22 per shoot, erect, flat, to 12cm x 3mm, pale green. Infl. to 30cm tall, branched, 12–26-flowered, each flower 12–16mm across, pale blue with darker nerves, tips occas. darker. NOTES: Uncommon sp. that forms dense clumps in small, scattered populations. FLOWERING: Sep–Oct. RANGE/HABITAT: WA (Mogumber to Busselton). Shallow freshwater claypans in shrubland.

SPIRAL-LEAVED SQUILL *Chamaescilla spiralis*

Flowering plant.

SIZE/ID: Dense tufting lily. Leaves more than 8 per shoot, to 15cm x 4mm, crowded, appressed to the ground, spirally twisted, dark green. Infl. to 40cm tall, branched, 20–100-flowered, each flower 12–16mm across, dark blue with darker nerves. NOTES: Distinctive spirally twisted leaves in a basal rosette. FLOWERING: Sep–Oct. RANGE/HABITAT: WA (Wongan Hills to Esperance). Woodland and shrubland in moist sandy soil.

BROAD-LEAVED SQUILL *Chamaescilla versicolor*

SIZE/ID: Clumping lily. Leaves 1–2 per shoot, erect or spreading, flat, to 25cm x 35mm, dark green. Infl. to 40cm tall, branched, 12–35-flowered, each flower 16–22mm across, dark blue with darker nerves. NOTES: Distinctive for its broad leaves. Widespread and common in WA. FLOWERING: Aug–Dec.
RANGE/HABITAT: WA (Kalbarri to Lake Grace). Woodland in loam and clay.

CLUB-FRUIT LILY *Corynotheca lateriflora*

SIZE/ID: Leaves to 12cm long, narrow. Infl. to 1m long, bush-like, much branched, erect to spreading, bright green. Flowers solitary, 10–15mm across, cream/white. Tepals narrow with darker central band, spreading or recurved. Capsules to 15mm long, erect. NOTES: The vast bulk of the plant consists of the strongly branched, shrub-like infl. FLOWERING: Feb–Jul; also sporadic.
RANGE/HABITAT: NT. Woodland, sandstone outcrops, stream banks, in sand.

NORTHERN FLAX LILY *Dianella atraxis*

SIZE/ID: Plants clumping. Stems to 1.5m long. Leaves to 1m x 4cm, flat, dark green, base occluded, margins finely toothed. Panicles longer than leaves, erect/arching, narrowly branched. Pedicels to 5mm long, persistent after flowers fall. Flowers crowded, 10–15mm across, mauve/blue with darker nerves. Filament swellings yellow. Anthers cream to pale yellow. Berries 6–8mm long, blue/purple.
FLOWERING: Aug–Mar.
RANGE/HABITAT: Qld (n). Wetter forests, including rainforest.

CROWDED FLAX LILY *Dianella caerulea* var. *vannata*

SIZE/ID: Plants clumping. Stems elongating, to 1.8m long, basal part with reduced scale-like leaves. Leaves to 75cm x 2.5cm, flat, dark green, base occluded. Panicles longer than leaves, erect/arching, narrowly branched. Pedicels to 8mm long. Flowers numerous, crowded, 10–15mm across, pale blue with prominent stamens. Filament swellings yellow/orange. Anthers yellow/orange. Berries 8–10mm long, blue/purple. FLOWERING: Aug–Mar. RANGE/HABITAT: Qld, NSW (Torres Strait Is. to Sydney); also NG. Lowlands to mountains in open forest.

BEACH FLAX LILY *Dianella congesta*

Fruit.

SIZE/ID: Dense spreading clumps. Stems to 60cm long. Leaves crowded, to 45cm x 15mm, flat, dark green, base occluded. Panicles to 35cm tall, arching/decurved, branching. Pedicels to 8mm long, winged. Flowers 2–8 per cluster, crowded, 15–20mm across, blue. Filament swellings bright yellow. Anthers yellow/brown. Berries 8–12mm long, globose, blue. NOTES: Flowers and fruit often borne together. FLOWERING: Apr–Aug.
RANGE/HABITAT: Qld, NSW (Rockhampton to Bermagui). Coastal forests and sand dunes.

PALE FLAX LILY *Dianella longifolia* var. *longifolia*

SIZE/ID: Plants solitary, tufted. Stems to 10cm long. Leaves to 80cm x 15mm, flat, dark green, base occluded. Panicles longer than leaves, erect/arching, branching. Pedicels to 20mm long. Flowers 12–20mm across, pale blue, white or greenish. Filament swellings orange. Anthers pale yellow. Berries 5–7mm long, blue. NOTES: Widely distributed variable sp. in need of study. FLOWERING: Aug–Mar.

RANGE/HABITAT: Qld (n to Cape York), NT, NSW, Vic, Tas, SA (se). Open forest and woodland.

NODDING FLAX LILY *Dianella rara*

SIZE/ID: Plants solitary, tufted. Leaves crowded, to 35cm x 5mm, flat, pale green, base red. Panicles to 80cm tall, arching, branching freely, branches widely divaricate. Pedicels to 30mm long, curved, pendent. Flowers 15–20mm across, pendent, blue or white. Filament swellings yellow/orange. Anthers cream/pale yellow. Berries 3–4mm long, blue. NOTES: Uncommon sp. with sporadic distribution. FLOWERING: Aug–Dec.
RANGE/HABITAT: Qld (Cooktown to Brisbane). Open forest and woodland.

TASMAN FLAX LILY *Dianella tasmanica*

SIZE/ID: Plants clumping/spreading. Stems to 10cm long. Leaves to 95cm x 3cm, flat, base occluded, dark green, margins recurved. Panicles as long as leaves, erect/arching, branched. Pedicels to 20mm long. Flowers 15–20mm across, lavender to blue. Filament swellings as long as anthers, golden. Anthers pale yellow. Berries 15–25mm long, dark blue/purple, shiny, often massed displays.
FLOWERING: Sep–Feb.
RANGE/HABITAT: NSW, Vic, Tas. Wetter forests, common at higher alt.

SCRAMBLING LILY *Geitonoplesium cymosum*

SIZE/ID: Monotypic genus in Aust., NG, Pacific Is. Climber with tough, wiry stems to 10m tall. Leaves to 10cm x 35mm, spreading, dark green, shiny, base twists into the petiole. Flowers in terminal groups, 10–22mm across, white to pale mauve with prominent yellow stamens. Tepals spreading widely, glabrous. Berries 10–20mm across, black. NOTES: Leaves are variable in width and shape. FLOWERING: Aug–Mar.
RANGE/HABITAT: Qld (n to Cape York), NSW, Vic. Wetter forests, including rainforest.

SKY LILY *Herpolirion novae-zelandiae*

SIZE/ID: Monotypic genus. Perennial lily forming mat-like ground-hugging clumps that spread by wiry rhizomes. Leaves in tufts, usually c.5 per stem, 4–6(–10)cm x 1.5–4mm, pale green/bluish. Flowers solitary, bisexual, c.4cm across, usually white, occas. bluish. Tepals 6, subequal, 2.5–3mm wide. Stamens 6, yellow. Filaments downy. Fruit a capsule. FLOWERING: Dec–Feb. RANGE/HABITAT: NSW, Vic, Tas; also NZ. Moist/wet peaty soil in alpine herbfield, heath and grassland above 1,200m alt.

DWARF HOODED LILY *Johnsonia acaulis*

SIZE/ID: Plants dwarfed, hairy. Roots often stilt-like. Leaves to 16cm x 3mm, green, prominently striate, hairy. Flower stem 2–6.5cm long with a terminal, upright, red or green infl. Floral bracts to 11 x 7mm, red or green, ovate, cupped, margins minutely hairy. Flowers 3–5mm long, white, pink or green. FLOWERING: Aug–Dec.
RANGE/HABITAT: WA (Perth to Israelite Bay). Forest, shrubland and heath in sand.

HOODED LILY *Johnsonia lupulina*

Flower heads.

SIZE/ID: Plants tussock-like, glabrous. Leaves to 75cm x 2mm, linear. Flower stem 40–70cm long with a terminal spreading to nodding white infl. Floral bracts to 24 x 6mm, white, lanceolate, cupped, pointed. Flowers 7–8mm long, white. FLOWERING: Sep–Nov.
RANGE/HABITAT: WA (Collie to Albany). Forest and woodland in sand.

PINK HOODED LILY *Johnsonia teretifolia*

SIZE/ID: Plants tussock-like, glabrous. Leaves to 40cm x 2mm, linear. Flower stem 40–50cm long with a terminal, nodding, pink infl. Floral bracts to 17 x 6mm, pink, lanceolate, cupped, pointed. Flowers 6–8mm long, purple. FLOWERING: Oct–Dec. RANGE/HABITAT: WA (Denmark to Stirling Ra.). Swamps and winter-wet flats in peaty sand and loam.

NODDING BLUE LILY *Stypandra glauca*

SIZE/ID: Stems to 1.5m tall, often with leafy branches. Leaves to 20cm x 15mm, erect to spreading, often partly twisted, green to bluish green, long-pointed. Flowers 15–30mm across, usually blue, occas. white. Tepals spreading or recurved. Stamens c.1cm long. Anthers yellow. Capsules 5–12mm long. NOTES: Variants in WA, some of which have been formally named, need further study.
FLOWERING: Aug–Jan.
RANGE/HABITAT: QLD (s), NSW, Vic, SA, WA. Drier forests and woodlands, often on rocky slopes.

TUFTED LILY *Thelionema caespitosum*

SIZE/ID: Plants to 1m tall. Tufts 5–20cm across at base. Leaves to 35cm x 12mm. Panicles to 80cm tall, with 2–3 major branches and 7 minor branches. Flowers 15–25mm across, starry, white, pale yellow, pale blue to deep blue or mixed blue and white. Anthers yellow. Capsules 5–10mm long. NOTES: Hybridises with other sp.
FLOWERING: Aug–Jan.
RANGE/HABITAT: QLD (se), NSW, Vic, Tas, SA, NT. Coast to high mountains in damp sand.

GRANITE LILY *Thelionema grande*

Buds and flower.

SIZE/ID: Plants to 1.3m tall. Tufts 10–25cm across at base. Leaves to 65cm x 28mm, crowded, flat, dark green to bluish green. Panicles to 1.3m tall, with 4–5 major branches and many minor branches. Flowers 20–30mm across, usually deep blue, occas. white. Anthers yellow. Capsules 8–10mm long. NOTES: Often on granite sheets or among boulders. FLOWERING: Oct–Dec.
RANGE/HABITAT: QLD, NSW (Stanthorpe to Howell). Forest in ranges above 800m alt.

LEMON TUFTED LILY *Thelionema umbellatum*

SIZE/ID: Plants to 40cm tall. Tufts 1–5cm across at base. Leaves appearing basal but alternate on a stem, to 35cm x 4mm, spreading, flat, green. Panicles 25–40cm tall, with 1–3 spreading branches. Flowers 8–15mm across, white or cream. Anthers yellow. Capsules 5–7mm long. FLOWERING: Oct–Dec.
RANGE/HABITAT: NSW (n to Swansea), Vic, Tas. Coast to 1,000m alt. in mountains; heath and forest in moist sand or peat.

WINGED RUSH LILY *Tricoryne anceps*

SIZE/ID: Leaves absent or short-lived, grass-like, to 30 x 4mm. Stems clustered, to 70cm x 5mm, flattened with wing-like margins. Flowers 12–24mm across, yellow, with prominent furry staminal filaments, in 3–15-flowered umbels. Sepals with 3–7 veins. Fruit 5–7mm long, strongly ribbed. FLOWERING: sporadic all year. RANGE/HABITAT: Qld (n to Cape York), NSW(n); also NG. Coast to ranges and tlnds in grassy forest, heath and on stony slopes.

YELLOW RUSH LILY *Tricoryne elatior*

SIZE/ID: Plant sub-shrubby to sprawling. Leaves short-lived, to 10cm x 3mm. Stems clustered, green, forking freely, to 90cm x 2mm. Flowers 10–20mm across, bright yellow, in 10–20-flowered umbels. Tepals with greenish central line. Sepals often brownish externally. NOTES: Occasionally grows in extensive swards.
FLOWERING: mainly Aug–May; also sporadic.
RANGE/HABITAT: Qld (n to Cairns), NSW, ACT, Vic Tas, SA (s), WA, NT. Coast to inland in forest, heath and grassland.

DWARF RUSH LILY *Tricoryne humilis*

SIZE/ID: Plants sprawling or prostrate, spreading by rhizomes. Leaves to 10cm x 7mm, green, often a few hairs. Stems to 40cm long, sparsely branched, angular. Flowers 12–20mm across, bright yellow, in 8–12-flowered umbels. Filament hairs orange.
FLOWERING: Sep–Jan.
RANGE/HABITAT: WA (Perth to Stirling Ra.). Coast to wheatbelt; forest and heath in sand and gravel, often moist.

SANDSTONE RUSH LILY *Tricoryne simplex*

SIZE/ID: Sprawling, prostrate or low growing clumps. Leaves to 25cm x 5mm, dark green, margins hairy. Stems to 30cm long, rarely branched, angular. Flowers 10–20mm across, bright yellow, in 6–20-flowered umbels. FLOWERING: Aug–Dec.
RANGE/HABITAT: NSW (Port Stephens to Nowra). Coastal forest and heath in sand over sandstone.

MALLEE RUSH LILY *Tricoryne tenella*

SIZE/ID: Plants erect, clumping. Leaves absent or reduced to small scales. Stems clustered, green, to 70cm long, terete, striate, grooved, forking freely. Flowers 10–18mm across, yellow or whitish, in 2–15-flowered umbels. FLOWERING: Aug–Jan.
RANGE/HABITAT: Vic (nw), SA (se, Kangaroo Is.), WA (Geraldton to Cape Arid). Coastal scrub on dunes; sand ridges in mallee heath; seasonally wet sites; usually in sand or gravel.

SHORT GRASSTREE *Xanthorrhoea acaulis*

SIZE/ID: Trunk usually absent, occas. to 30cm tall, often branched below ground. Leaves 1.5–1.8mm wide, c.1mm thick, grey/green. Infl. to 70cm long, sturdy; woody scape to 45cm x 12mm; flower spike 10–25 x 2.5–3.5cm. Flowers white. FLOWERING: Jul–Dec. RANGE/HABITAT: NSW (Narrabri to Grenfell). Scrubby forest in sand.

SOUTHERN GRASSTREE *Xanthorrhoea australis*

After fire.

SIZE/ID: Trunk to 3m tall, single or branched. Leaves 1.2–3mm wide, 1–2.2mm thick, bluish/grey. Infl. to 3m long; woody scape to 50 x 4cm; flower spike 1–2.5m x 5–8cm. Flowers white.
FLOWERING: Nov–Jan.
RANGE/HABITAT: NSW (s of Nowra), Vic, Tas, SA (se). Coastal forest, swamps and heath.

BOTTLEBRUSH GRASSTREE *Xanthorrhoea macronema*

SIZE/ID: Trunk absent, often branched below ground to form multi-crowned clump. Leaves 2.5–3.5mm wide, 1.2–1.8mm thick, green. Infl. to 1.8m long; woody scape to 160cm x 5mm; flower spike brush-like, 5–13 x 1.5–2cm. Flowers cream/yellowish. FLOWERING: Jul–Jan.

RANGE/HABITAT: Qld, NSW (Fraser Is. to Sydney). Coastal scrub and heath in sand.

SMALL GRASSTREE *Xanthorrhoea minor*

SIZE/ID: Trunk absent, branching below ground to form multi-crowned clump. Leaves erect, 2–3.5mm wide, 1–1.5mm thick, green. Infl. to 1m long; woody scape to 60cm x 15mm; flower spike 5–30 x 1–2.5cm. Flowers cream/yellowish.. NOTES: *X. minor* subsp. *minor* is restricted to NSW, subsp. *lutea* occurs in Vic and se SA.
FLOWERING: Oct–Apr.
RANGE/HABITAT: NSW, Vic, SA. Heathy forest and heath in sand.

DWARF GRASSTREE *Xanthorrhoea nana*

SIZE/ID: Trunk usually absent, occas. to 50cm tall, branching below ground to form multi-crowned clump. Leaves stiffly erect, spiky, 2.5–3mm wide, 1.5–2mm thick, blue/green. Infl. to 80cm long, emerging horizontally then curved upwards; woody scape to 40cm x 15mm; flower spike 25–35 x 2.5–5cm. Flowers white. FLOWERING: Sep–Oct.
RANGE/HABITAT: WA (Lake Grace to Lake Moore). Mallee shrubland and heath in yellow sand and sandy clay.

PINEAPPLE GRASS *Astelia alpina* var. *novae-hollandiae*

Fruit.

SIZE/ID: Spreading clumps. Leaves to 17cm x 15mm, bright green with silvery scales. Female panicles nestling among leaves, 1–2.5cm long. Female flowers c.1cm across, crowded, yellowish. Male panicles exserted above leaves, 3–8cm long. Male flowers 4–8mm across. Berries 6–10mm long, orange/red. NOTES: Often prominent after bushfires. FLOWERING: Nov–Mar. RANGE/HABITAT: NSW, Vic. Common above c.1,350m alt. in alpine bogs, mossbeds and herbfields.

ROBUST PINEAPPLE GRASS *Astelia psychrocharis*

SIZE/ID: Spreading mats. Most parts with silvery scales and silky hairs. Leaves to 20cm x 4cm, grey green on both sides. Panicles compact, nestling or hidden among leaves, c.2cm long. Flowers 15–20mm across, crowded, reddish. Berries 9–18mm long, orange/yellow. FLOWERING: Nov–Mar.
RANGE/HABITAT: NSW (Kosciuszko area), Vic (Mt Wellington). Alpine herbfields and near streams.

LINDON'S LILY *Milligania lindoniana*

SIZE/ID: Plants clumping. Leaves 5–20cm x 1–2cm, green above, greyish to silvery white beneath, with appressed hairs and pale scales. Panicles erect, hairy, 5–20cm long with 2–6 branches (occas. a short raceme). Flowers crowded, 10–18mm across, white with dark red tube and tepal bases. Capsules 5–7mm long.
FLOWERING: Dec–Jan.
RANGE/HABITAT: Tas (s, w). Among cushion plants and herbs on mountains in moist/wet peaty soil.

LEDGE LILY *Milligania stylosa*

SIZE/ID: Plants clumping. Leaves 15–50cm x 2–3.5cm, green with scattered pale scales. Panicles erect, hairy, 2–8cm long with 2–6 branches. Flowers crowded, 10–15mm across, white; tepals reflexing to expose developing capsules. Anthers cream on white filaments. Capsules 2–3mm long. FLOWERING: Dec–Jan. RANGE/HABITAT: Tas (s, w). Seepage sites on exposed cliffs, rocky clefts and ledges, above 900m alt.

SILVER SWORD LILY *Neoastelia spectabilis*

SIZE/ID: Endemic monotypic genus. Plants clumping. Leaves to 1.6m x 6cm, green above, silvery white beneath, tips drooping. Panicles 25–70cm long, sturdy, hairy. Flowers bisexual, crowded, 15–18mm across, whitish. Perianth segments 10, 12 or 14, membranous. Stamens 10–14. Berries 11–15mm long, pale green. NOTES: Very rare sp. FLOWERING: Nov–Dec.
RANGE/HABITAT: NSW (ne). Above 900m alt. in rock crevices on steep slopes; beside waterfalls and seepage areas on rocky slopes.

BLUE MOUNTAINS BELLS *Blandfordia cunninghamii*

SIZE/ID: Leaves to 1m x 12mm, rush-like, bright green, margins smooth, recurved, with transparent band. Racemes to 80cm tall, 12–30-flowered. Flowers to 6 x 4cm, red with yellow tips, narrow at base then abruptly expanded and bell-like to apex. Capsules to 8cm long. FLOWERING: Dec–Apr.

RANGE/HABITAT: NSW (mainly Blue Mtns, Illawarra scarp). Damp areas and peaty soils on sandstone near streams and cliff edges.

CHRISTMAS BELLS *Blandfordia grandiflora*

Yellow flowers.

SIZE/ID: Leaves grass-like, to 70cm x 5mm, bright green, flat, channelled, underside keeled, margins roughened. Raceme to 1.8m tall, 2–20-flowered. Flowers to 6 x 4cm, red with yellow tips or wholly yellow, apex widening or flared. Capsules to 6cm long. NOTES: Forms sporadic hybrids with *B. nobilis*. FLOWERING: Nov–Feb.

RANGE/HABITAT: Qld, NSW (Gympie to Hawkesbury R.). Coast to tlnds in damp/wet heath in sandy or peaty soil.

SMALL CHRISTMAS BELLS *Blandfordia nobilis*

SIZE/ID: Leaves grass-like, to 60cm x 5mm bright green, channelled, underside keeled, margins smooth or roughened. Racemes to 80cm tall, 3–20-flowered. Flowers to 3.5 x 2cm, red with yellow tips, narrow at base then expanded and tubular/cylindrical. Capsules to 6cm long. NOTES: Forms sporadic hybrids with *B. grandiflora*.
FLOWERING: Nov–Jan.
RANGE/HABITAT: NSW (Sydney to Milton, inland to Blue Mtns and Braidwood). Coast to ranges on wet slopes over sandstone and swampy heath.

TASMANIAN CHRISTMAS BELLS *Blandfordia punicea*

SIZE/ID: Leaves to 1m x 8mm, flat, ribbed, green or reddish, margins with small teeth. Racemes to 1m tall, 15–50-flowered. Flowers to 4.5 x 2cm, red externally, yellow internally, narrow at base then uniformly and narrowly expanded. Capsules to 4cm long.
FLOWERING: Oct–Feb.
RANGE/HABITAT: Tas (mainly w). Lowlands to mountains in heaths and button grass moorland.

SANDSTONE LILY *Alania cunninghamii*

SIZE/ID: Endemic monotypic genus. Clumping/sprawling perennial herb with wiry stems to 30cm tall, rooting at nodes. Leaves spirally arranged, crowded, stiff, 2–12cm x 0.5mm. Dense heads of 20–30 flowers are carried on a long thin scape. Flowers bisexual, 4–6mm across, white. Stamens protruding; filaments white, filiform; anthers orange/yellow. Fruit a globose capsule. FLOWERING: Dec–Mar. RANGE/HABITAT: NSW (mainly Blue Mtns, also Gosford to Camden). Crevices and ledges on moist sandstone rock faces.

PINCUSHIONS *Borya nitida*

Flowering plant.

SIZE/ID: Dome-like perennial herb to 15cm high. Leaves needle-like, crowded, 10–20mm x c.1mm, green, stiff, tip yellowish, sharply pointed. Heads of crowded flowers to 1cm across carried on scapes to 5cm long. Flowers 3–4mm across, white. NOTES: Plants can resurrect after drying out and appearing dead. FLOWERING: Jun–Oct.

RANGE/HABITAT: WA (Albany to Israelite Bay). Exposed granite outcrops, rock sheets and bare sand.

PORCUPINE LILY *Borya septentrionalis*

SIZE/ID: Clumping/sprawling herb with wiry stems to 45cm tall. Leaves needle-like, rigid, crowded, 3–50mm x 1mm, green, tip black, sharply pointed. Heads of crowded flowers to 2cm across carried on scapes to 24cm long. Flowers 4–6mm across, white. NOTES: Resurrection plant, clumps turn orange when dry. FLOWERING: Dec–Apr.
RANGE/HABITAT: Qld (Mossman to Cardwell Ra., Hinchinbrook Is.). Shallow soil on sunny rock outcrops, rubble, rock sheets and platforms.

ALISON'S MILKMAIDS *Burchardia bairdiae*

SIZE/ID: Leaves 2–4, basal. Scape to 120cm tall, usually branched (occas. unbranched), uppermost bract to 30mm long. Buds pink or pinkish white. Flowers in groups of 5–22, each flower 20–25mm across, white or pinkish. Anthers yellow. Capsules not thickened on angles. FLOWERING: Aug–Nov.
RANGE/HABITAT: WA (Jurien Bay to Jandakot). Winter-wet swamps in peaty soil.

CROWDED MILKMAIDS *Burchardia congesta*

SIZE/ID: Leaves 1 or 2, basal. Scape to 80cm tall, usually unbranched or with 1 branch, uppermost bract to 40mm long. Buds whitish with pink markings. Flowers in groups of 2–9, each flower 20–25mm across, white. Anthers yellow. Capsules with conspicuous glossy thickenings on angles. FLOWERING: Aug–Oct. RANGE/HABITAT: WA (Northampton to Stirling Ra.). Shrubby forest on sand dunes, plains, ridges and slopes in various soils.

SINGLE MILKMAID *Burchardia monantha*

SIZE/ID: Leaf 1. Scape to 34cm tall, unbranched, pinkish, with 3 bracts 5–10mm long. Buds pink. Flower single, white to pale pink, 16–22mm across. Tepals with darker pink external stripe. Anthers yellow. Capsules not thickened on angles. FLOWERING: Sep–Nov. RANGE/HABITAT: WA (Manjimup to Cranbrook). Forest, winter-wet swamps and seepage areas.

WESTERN MILKMAIDS *Burchardia multiflora*

Pinkish flowers.

SIZE/ID: Leaves 2, basal. Scape to 27cm tall, unbranched or branched, uppermost bract to 160mm long. Buds deep pink. Flowers in groups of 3–20, each flower 20–25mm across, white or pinkish. Tepals with external pink stripe. Anthers purple. Capsules dull, slightly thickened on angles. FLOWERING: Jul–Sep. RANGE/HABITAT: WA (Jurien Bay to Stirling Ra.). Winter-wet swamps, margins of granite outcrops, streambanks, shallow soil and moss over rock plates.

PINK MILKMAIDS *Burchardia rosea*

SIZE/ID: Leaves 4–5, basal. Scape to 50cm tall, unbranched or sparsely branched, uppermost bract to 40mm long. Buds deep pink. Flowers in groups of 3–8, each flower 20–25mm across, opening bright pink, fading with age. Anthers yellow. Capsules not thickened on angles. FLOWERING: Aug–Oct.
RANGE/HABITAT: WA (Kalbarri to Port Gregory). Winter-wet swamps, moist flats, margins of granite outcrops.

EASTERN MILKMAIDS *Burchardia umbellata*

SIZE/ID: Leaves 1 or 2, basal. Scape to 65cm tall, usually unbranched or with 1 branch, uppermost bract to 40mm long. Buds greenish to white. Flowers in groups of 2–9, each flower 20–25mm across, white. Tepals with faint pink external stripe. Anthers purple. Capsules without thickenings on angles. NOTES: Roots are reportedly edible raw. FLOWERING: Aug–Oct. RANGE/HABITAT: Qld (s from Fraser Is.), NSW, Vic, Tas, SA (w to Eyre Pen.). Forest, woodland, shrubland, heath, rocky outcrops.

STAR LILY *Iphigenia indica*

SIZE/ID: Plants slender, to 50cm tall. Leaves 3–6, to 20cm x 4.5mm, green. Stem thin, single or branching. Flowers 1–4, 12–20mm across, star-like, dark red to reddish/brown. Tepals spreading widely, thin. Capsules to 20 x 5mm, upright. NOTES: Inconspicuous and easily overlooked. FLOWERING: Jan–Mar.
RANGE/HABITAT: Qld, NSW (n), NT (n), WA (n). Open forest and woodland in well-drained soil.

WHITE FOREST LILY *Schelhammera multiflora*

SIZE/ID: Small clumps to 40cm tall. Stems erect to sprawling. Leaves to 80 x 4cm, bright green, veins raised, margins minutely hairy. Cymes terminal, multiflowered, 1 flower open at a time. Flowers 10–20mm across, white, scented. Tepals with incurved margins. Capsule on decurved stalk, 5–8mm diam., wrinkled, yellow/brown when ripe. FLOWERING: Feb–Oct.
RANGE/HABITAT: Qld (Cape York to Ingham); also NG. Sea level to mountains in eucalypt forest and rainforest margins.

LILAC LILY *Schelhammera undulata*

SIZE/ID: Small suckering clumps to 20cm tall. Stems erect to sprawling. Leaves to 50 x 18mm, dark green, margins wavy. Flower solitary, 10–15mm across, pink/mauve. Tepals 2–4mm wide, spreading, tips recurved. Capsule 5–8mm diam., wrinkled. NOTES: Sporadic in small patches. FLOWERING: Sep–Nov. RANGE/HABITAT: NSW, Vic (Lismore to East Gippsland). Sheltered sites in coastal scrubs and wetter forests.

KREYSIGIA *Tripladenia cunninghamii*

SIZE/ID: Endemic monotypic genus. Spreading, suckering clumps to 40cm tall. Stems erect to arching. Leaves to 70 x 25mm, dark green, shiny, veins prominent. Flowers in 1- or few-flowered axillary groups, 20–25mm across, pink/mauve. Tepals 4–7mm wide, margins wavy. Capsule 6–8mm diam., wrinkled. NOTES: Sporadic, sometimes locally common. FLOWERING: Oct–Mar. RANGE/HABITAT: Qld, NSW (Noosa to Myall Lakes). Sheltered sites in rainforest and other wetter forests.

COMMON NANCY *Wurmbea biglandulosa*

SIZE/ID: Plants to 30cm tall. Leaves 3, evenly spaced, 1–3mm wide, dark green, shiny. Flowers 1–6, bisexual (occas. unisexual), 16–20mm across, usually white, occas. pink. Tepals with 2 white/pink shelf-like marginal nectaries one third from base. Filaments 3–5mm long. Anthers red/purple. FLOWERING: Aug–Nov. RANGE/HABITAT: Qld, NSW, Vic (Nambour to Wulgulmerang). Widespread and common in forest, moist grassy areas and among rocks.

ROCK NANCY *Wurmbea centralis*

SIZE/ID: Plants to 20cm tall. Leaves 3, 2 closer together at base, spreading, 18–24mm wide, leathery, dark green, shiny. Flowers 1–10, bisexual, 18–24mm across, bright pink. Tepals with 2 darker pink ledge-like nectaries one third from base, apex pointed. Filaments 5–10mm long. Anthers purplish. Capsules swollen, papery. FLOWERING: May–Aug.
RANGE/HABITAT: NT, SA. Semi-arid inland areas among rocks.

YELLOW NANCY *Wurmbea citrina*

Male (left) and female plants.

Male flowers.

SIZE/ID: Plants to 30cm tall. Leaves 3, evenly spaced, 3–15mm wide, leathery. Plants ♂ or ♀. Flowers 5–20, 12–16mm across, yellow/green (♂ plants with to 20 larger flowers). Tepals with 1 brownish transverse nectary band one third from base. Filaments 3–4mm long. Anthers purple/brown. FLOWERING: May–Sep. RANGE/HABITAT: NSW (w), SA. Semi-arid inland *Callitris* woodland in sand or sand over clay.

CROWDED NANCY *Wurmbea densiflora*

SIZE/ID: Plants to 20cm tall. Leaves 3, 2 closer together at base, 2–7mm wide, green. Flowers 2–10, bisexual, crowded, 18–25mm across, whitish to bright pink. Tepals with 2 small, inconspicuous, swollen, pink or whitish marginal nectaries one third from base. Filaments 6–9mm long. Anthers pink/purple or yellow.
FLOWERING: May–Sep.
RANGE/HABITAT: WA (Murchison R. to Leonora to Nungarin). Shrubland in sand or sand over clay.

HARBINGER OF SPRING, EARLY NANCY

Wurmbea dioica

Male plant and two females.

SIZE/ID: Plants to 30cm tall. Leaves 3, evenly spaced, 0.5–3mm wide, dark green, shiny. Plants ♂ or ♀. Flowers 1–11, 8–20mm across, white (♂ plants with larger flowers). Tepals with 1 purplish transverse nectary band quarter to halfway from base. Filaments 3–8mm long. Anthers red/purple. NOTES: Widespread, common but variable sp. Often forms massed displays. FLOWERING: Jun–Nov. RANGE/HABITAT: Qld, NSW, Vic, Tas, SA. Often in moist grassy areas but also in drier sites among shrubs and trees.

DRUMMOND'S NANCY *Wurmbea drummondii*

Male plants.

SIZE/ID: Plants to 5cm tall. Leaves 3, 2 closer together at base, 5–18mm wide, leathery. Plants ♂ or ♀. Flowers 2–7, 5–7mm long, white (ageing pink) to bright pink (♂ plants with open infl., ♀ dense). Tepals with 1 white to dark pink, curved, transverse nectary band one third from base. Filaments 3–5mm long. Anthers purple.
FLOWERING: Jun–Jul.
RANGE/HABITAT: WA (n of Moora to near Lake Grace). Forest and shrubland in sand and clay.

GASCOYNE NANCY *Wurmbea inflata*

SIZE/ID: Plants to 15cm tall. Leaves 2, both close together at base, 4–16mm wide, broadly channelled, dark green, shiny. Flowers 1–2(–3), bisexual, 15–20mm across, pink, occas. white. Tepals 8, occas. 6 or 7, with 1 inconspicuous nectary 2mm from base. Anthers yellow or dark red. Capsules large, papery. NOTES: Only flowers in years of good rainfall. FLOWERING: May–Jun. RANGE/HABITAT: WA (Kennedy Ra. to e of Mt Augustus). Sparse shrubland on rocky hills in red loam.

MURCHISON RIVER NANCY *Wurmbea murchisoniana*

SIZE/ID: Plants to 26cm tall. Leaves 3, evenly spaced, 1–4mm wide, dark green, shiny. Flowers 1–7, bisexual, 14–22mm across, white. Tepals with 2 white, ledge-like, thickened, marginal nectaries one third from base. Filaments 3–5mm long. Anthers dark red. NOTES: Occas. in massed floral displays. FLOWERING: Jul–Aug. RANGE/HABITAT: WA (lower Murchison R.). Winter-wet hollows in shrubland over clay.

BARLEE RANGE NANCY *Wurmbea saccata*

SIZE/ID: Plants to 30cm tall. Leaves 3 or 4, unevenly spaced, to 15cm x 14mm, dark green, shiny. Flowers 5–14, bisexual, 20–25mm across, sweetly scented, pale pink, occas. white. Tepals with nectaries in basal pouch-like structures. Filaments 6–6.5mm long. Anthers yellow or red. NOTES: Specialised sp. that grows in an arid area with low and irregular rainfall. FLOWERING: Jun. RANGE/HABITAT: WA (Barlee Ra. se. of Onslow). Creek lines and rock pools in sandstone hills.

TUBULAR NANCY *Wurmbea tubulosa*

Male plants.

SIZE/ID: Plants to 3cm tall. Leaves 3, 2 close together at base, 5–22mm wide, dark green. Plants ♂ or ♀. Flowers 1–16, white or pink, ♂ 6–7mm long, ♀ 9–12mm long, base tubular. Tepals fused in basal half, with 1 white/pink, curved, transverse nectary band midway from base. Filaments 4–8mm long. Anthers purple/red.
FLOWERING: Jul–Aug.
RANGE/HABITAT: WA (near Greenough, near Mingenew). Shrubland on riverbanks and winter-wet areas.

SINGLE NANCY *Wurmbea uniflora*

SIZE/ID: Plants to 17cm tall. Leaves 3, evenly spaced, 1–2mm wide, dark green. Flower single (occas. 2), bisexual, 10–15mm across, white. Tepals with 2 shelf–like, marginal nectaries one third from base. Filaments 3–5mm long. Anthers red/brown. FLOWERING: Sep–Jan.

RANGE/HABITAT: NSW (se, rare), Vic, Tas, SA (se, rare). Localised and generally uncommon in moist/wet grassy areas, swamps and button grass plains.

YELLOW DAYLILY *Cartonema spicatum*

SIZE/ID: Perennial herb 10–35cm tall. Leaves to 40cm x 7mm, concave, hairy, bright green. Racemes 1–4, 4–30cm tall, stem glandular-hairy. Flowers 20–32mm across. Sepals 10–16mm long, green, acuminate. Petals 10–16mm long, widest near apex, flimsy, yellow or white. Capsules 5–7mm long, glandular-hairy.
FLOWERING: Jan–Jul.
RANGE/HABITAT: Tropical Qld, NT, WA. Woodland, grassland and sandstone formations, often in moist sand.

SCURVY WEED *Commelina ensifolia*

SIZE/ID: Stems spreading. Leaves ovate, to 13cm x 25mm, bright green. Spathes minutely hairy. Sepals 4–6mm long. Flowers 20–25mm across, bright blue, 2 petals much larger than third. Capsule enclosed in large, curled bract. FLOWERING: Sporadic all year. RANGE/HABITAT: Qld, NSW, SA, NT, WA; also Asia. Moist areas in forest, grassland, rocky slopes and near streams.

GRASS LILY *Murdannia graminea*

SIZE/ID: Perennial herb with thick fleshy roots. Leaves to 30cm x 10mm, bright green, somewhat roughened. Panicles 20–60cm tall. Sepals 6–8mm long. Flowers 10–20mm across, pale blue, mauve or white. Capsules 6–10mm long, enclosed by sepals. NOTES: Roots are reportedly edible raw. FLOWERING: Dec–May. RANGE/HABITAT: Qld, NSW, NT, WA. Moist to wet soil in grassy forest, swamps and near streams.

LARGE-FLOWERED TINSEL LILY *Calectasia grandiflora*

SIZE/ID: Plants with rhizomes, no stilt roots. Stems to 65cm tall, freely branching. Leaves to 16 x 5mm, sharply pointed. Flowers with a basal tube c.1cm long, 20–40mm across, blue, ageing red, lobes tapered to a sharp point. Anthers yellow, not ageing orange/red. NOTES: Variable sp. Typical variant is from Perth region, other variants from Wheatbelt and South Coast. FLOWERING: Jul–Sep. RANGE/HABITAT: WA (Perth region). Wet heath.

STAR OF BETHLEHEM *Calectasia narragara*

SIZE/ID: Plants with short rhizomes, no stilt roots. Stems to 50cm tall, freely branching. Leaves to 14 x 5mm, blunt with a short central point. Flowers with a basal tube c.1cm long, 18–25mm across, blue with bronze margins, ageing white, lobes tapered to a sharp point. Anthers yellow, ageing orange/red. NOTES: Resprouts after fire. FLOWERING: Jun–Sep.
RANGE/HABITAT: WA (Geraldton to Busselton). Sandplain, woodland, occas. swampy sites.

PINEAPPLE BUSH *Dasypogon bromeliifolius*

SIZE/ID: Stems to 1m tall. Clumps grass-like. Leaves to 55cm x 5mm, green, margins roughened. Flowers white, crowded in prickly ball-shaped heads 25–35mm across on the end of sturdy scapes. NOTES: Sharply pointed bracts extend out from the cluster of flowers. FLOWERING: Sep–Jan.
RANGE/HABITAT: WA (Moore R. to Fitzgerald R.). Wet flats in low woodland in sand.

BULLANOCK *Kingia australis*

Leaves and flower heads.

SIZE/ID: Monotypic genus in WA. Trunk 4–8m tall, unbranched, usually black from fire. Leaves narrow in a green crown, old leaves forming a grey/brown basal skirt. Flowers small, yellow/green/brown, densely crowded in globular, stalked heads. NOTES: Slow-growing species with similar appearance to a grasstree. Its pseudotrunk consists of old leaf bases and contains thin internal roots which absorb rain and nutrients. FLOWERING: Jul–Aug (after fire).

RANGE/HABITAT: WA (Kalbarri to Albany). Open forest.

GYMEA LILY *Doryanthes excelsa*

Flowers and New Holland Honeyeater.

SIZE/ID: Leaves to 2.5m x 10cm. Infl. to 5m tall, with short spreading stem leaves and a terminal globular head 50–70cm across of crowded flowers surrounded by brown bracts. Flowers 10–15cm long, red, paler within, rarely white. Tepals 6–12cm long, spreading widely at maturity. Capsule 7–10cm long, brown. NOTES: Commonly grown imposing plant. FLOWERING: Sep–Dec. RANGE/HABITAT: NSW (mainly Karuah to Mt Keira, disjunct at Glenreagh). Drier forest and sandstone country, with good drainage.

GIANT SPEAR LILY *Doryanthes palmeri*

SIZE/ID: Leaves to 3m x 20cm. Infl. to 5m long, spreading/arching, with short appressed stem leaves and an extended, one-sided head to 1.2m long. Flowers up to 350 per head, crowded, 6–12cm long, upright, red, paler within. Capsule 7–9cm long, brown. FLOWERING: Aug–Dec.
RANGE/HABITAT: Qld (se), NSW (n from Mt Warning). Exposed rock outcrops along cliff tops surrounded by wetter forest.

LITTLE KANGAROO PAW *Anigozanthos bicolor*

SIZE/ID: Leaves flat, to 35cm x 10mm, glabrous, green. Infl. 10–40cm tall, often unbranched, stem covered in red hairs. Flowers curved, 45–75mm long, mostly green, pedicels and base of flowers covered in red hairs. Tepal lobes 7–12mm long, recurved. Stamens protruding. FLOWERING: Aug–Oct.
RANGE/HABITAT: WA (Moora to Albany, Esperance). Winter-wet soils in woodland, heath and shrubland.

TALL KANGAROO PAW *Anigozanthos flavidus*

SIZE/ID: Leaves flat, to 100cm x 20mm, glabrous, dark green. Panicles 1–3m tall, stem mostly glabrous. Flowers straight or curved, 30–45mm long, yellowish green to brownish red. Tepal lobes 7.5–12mm long. FLOWERING: Nov–Jan.
RANGE/HABITAT: WA (Waroona to Two Peoples Bay). Moist sand and gravel in swamp margins, gutters and drainage lines in forest, heath and shrubland.

COMMON CAT'S PAW *Anigozanthos humilis*

SIZE/ID: Leaves flat, to 20cm x 15mm, glabrous, green, often recurved. Infl. 10–40cm tall, often unbranched, stem covered in reddish or greenish hairs. Pedicels and flowers covered in red and yellow hairs (flowers occas. all yellow). Flowers straight, 25–50mm long. Tepal lobes 4–13mm long. NOTES: Flowers best after fire.
FLOWERING: Jul–Oct.
RANGE/HABITAT: WA (Kalbarri to Hopetoun). Well-drained sand in mallee, heath and shrubland.

RED-AND-GREEN KANGAROO PAW

Anigozanthos manglesii

SIZE/ID: Leaves flat, 10–40cm x 5–12mm, glabrous, greyish green. Infl. 30–110cm tall, often unbranched, stem with sparse reddish hairs. Flowers curved, 6–10cm long, to 20mm wide, mostly verdant green, pedicels and base of flowers densely covered in red hairs. Tepal lobes 8–16mm long, reflexed. NOTES: Floral emblem of WA. FLOWERING: Aug–Nov.
RANGE/HABITAT: WA (Lancelin to Mount Barker). Well-drained sand in mallee, heath and shrubland.

ALBANY CAT'S PAW *Anigozanthos preissii*

SIZE/ID: Leaves nearly terete or keeled, to 25cm x 5mm, glabrous, green, most replaced annually. Infl. 20–70cm tall, stem covered in reddish hairs. Flowers straight, 50–60mm long, mostly yellow, pedicels and base of flowers covered in red hairs. Tepal lobes 14–22mm long, spreading widely. NOTES: Flowers best after fire.
FLOWERING: Oct–Nov.
RANGE/HABITAT: WA (Mount Barker to Two Peoples Bay). Sandy slopes in open woodland.

RED KANGAROO PAW *Anigozanthos rufus*

SIZE/ID: Leaves flat, to 40cm x 6mm, glabrous, greyish green to dark green. Panicles 50–100cm tall, stem hairy. Flowers straight, 25–35mm long, red to purplish. Tepal lobes 8.5–12.5mm long.
FLOWERING: Sep–Dec.
RANGE/HABITAT: WA (Stirling Ra. to Israelite Bay). Seasonally wet flats and drainage lines in heath and mallee.

WINTER BELL *Blancoa canescens*

SIZE/ID: Monotypic genus endemic in WA. Plants in tufts. Leaves in fans, to 25cm x 3mm, light green to grey green, flat, when young covered with short silky hairs. Racemes 15–25cm long. Flowers pendulous, 25–35mm long, tubular with short spreading lobes, densely covered with short red hairs. Fruit a capsule. NOTES: Distinctive sp. with attractive, colourful flowers. FLOWERING: Jun–Aug.
RANGE/HABITAT: WA (Eneabba to Moore R.). *Banksia* shrubland and heath in deep sand.

YELLOW TRUMPETS *Conostylis bealiana*

SIZE/ID: Leaves in fans, to 15cm x 2mm, green, flat, fine marginal hairs. Flowers single, arising among the leaves, 25–45mm long, tubular with spreading tips, showy, yellow to orange, rarely reddish or purplish. NOTES: Recognised by its colourful trumpet-like flowers. FLOWERING: Jul–Sep.

RANGE/HABITAT: WA (Fitzgerald R. to Israelite Bay). Mallee heath in sandy loam and gravel.

GREY COTTONHEADS

Conostylis candicans subsp. *procumbens*

SIZE/ID: Sprawling clumps spreading widely by stolons. Leaves in broad fans, to 20cm x 4mm, grey-hairy, flat. Infl. 12–32cm long, stalk grey, occas. branched near top. Flowers in densely crowded terminal clusters, each flower 8–12mm long, golden yellow, tepals not spreading widely. FLOWERING: Aug–Nov.
RANGE/HABITAT: WA (lower Irwin R.). Woodland and heath.

DEPRESSED CONOSTYLIS *Conostylis misera*

SIZE/ID: Prostrate clumps spreading by rhizomes. Leaves in small tufts, to 18cm x 6mm, flat, soft, green, glabrous, erect to spreading. Infl. 5–20mm long. Flower single, 12–19mm long, 20–25mm across, starry, yellow centrally, tepals paler. NOTES: Rare sp. Floral segments enlarge in fruit. FLOWERING: Oct–Nov. RANGE/HABITAT: WA (Mount Barker to Stirling Ra.). Winter-wet flats in mallee and heath.

SPREADING COTTONHEADS *Conostylis prolifera*

SIZE/ID: Small fan-like tufts of leaves connected by a network of stolons and forming spreading clumps. Leaves to 6cm x 1.5mm, green, flat. Infl. 1–15cm long, greyish, often sprawling. Flowers in densely crowded terminal clusters, each flower 7–13mm long, yellow/brown. Tepals not spreading widely. FLOWERING: Aug–Oct. RANGE/HABITAT: WA (Murchison R. to Beverley). Winter-wet flats in woodland and shrubland in clay loam.

MATTING CONOSTYLIS *Conostylis seorsiflora*

SIZE/ID: Prostrate mats, spreading by rhizomes. Leaves in small fans, to 16cm x 1.6mm, flat, green, glabrous. Infl. 1–5cm long. Flower single, 12–15mm long, 15–20mm across, starry, yellow centrally, tepals paler. FLOWERING: Sep–Dec.
RANGE/HABITAT: WA (Tambellup to Cape Arid). Winter-wet flats and seepage sites in woodland and mallee.

BRISTLY COTTONHEADS *Conostylis setigera*

Leaves and flowers.

SIZE/ID: Tufts to 20cm across. Leaves erect to spreading, to 36cm x 4mm, flat, striate, green with several ranks of prominent silvery-white marginal hairs 1–4.5mm long. Infl. 4–20cm long, with a cluster of 5–10 flowers, each flower 10–15mm long, 10–20mm across, yellow centrally, red with age, tepals paler. FLOWERING: Aug–Nov.

RANGE/HABITAT: WA (Gillingarra to Cape Arid). Woodland, forest and heath in sand and gravel.

WHITE COTTONHEADS *Conostylis setosa*

SIZE/ID: Small tufts. Leaves erect to spreading, to 30cm x 4mm, flat, striate, green with few ranks of white marginal hairs 1–5mm long. Infl. 8–35cm long. Flowers in dense terminal clusters, each flower 12–20mm long, 10–20mm across, starry, white, pinkish or purple, silky hairy. FLOWERING: Sep–Nov.
RANGE/HABITAT: WA (Bindoon to Dwellingup). Jarrah forest in laterite.

SHEATH CONOSTYLIS *Conostylis vaginata*

SIZE/ID: Compact tufts. Leaves erect to spreading, to 15cm x 1.5mm, terete, green, mostly glabrous, base hairy. Infl. sessile at base of leaves. Flowers few per group, each flower 10–13mm long, 8–12mm across, starry, golden yellow with white anthers.
FLOWERING: Sep–Oct.
RANGE/HABITAT: WA (Stirling Ra. to Esperance). Mallee and heath in well-drained sand.

SCARLET BLOODROOT *Haemodorum coccineum*

SIZE/ID: Winter dormant resprouter. Rootstock fleshy, red. Leaves flat, to 60cm x 10mm, greyish green. Panicles 50–150cm tall. Flowers crowded in a compact terminal head, not opening widely, 6–8mm long, flask-shaped, bright orange/scarlet, tips darker. Anthers just protruding. NOTES: Red dye is extracted from roots and flowers. FLOWERING: Nov–Mar.
RANGE/HABITAT: Tropical Qld (s to Mackay), NT (n). Forest and woodland.

BLACK KANGAROO PAW *Macropidia fuliginosa*

SIZE/ID: Monotypic genus endemic in WA. Leaves flat, in fans, to 50cm x 15mm, glabrous, bluish green. Panicles 50–180cm tall, stem covered in black hairs. Flowers curved, 5–6cm long, yellowish green, black hairs externally. Tepal lobes 8.5–12.5mm long, recurved or curled. Stamens protruding strongly. NOTES: Distinctive sp. with striking flowers. FLOWERING: Aug–Sep. RANGE/HABITAT: WA (Muchea to Walkaway). Mallee heath and heath in laterite.

STARRY GRASS LILY *Phlebocarya ciliata*

SIZE/ID: Clumps grass-like. Leaves to 65cm x 3.5mm, green, margins hairy. Panicles usually shorter than leaves, branches spreading. Flowers 6–10mm across, starry, cream/white with pink/red anthers. NOTES: Flowering plants superficially resemble a species of *Lomandra*. FLOWERING: Sep–Nov.
RANGE/HABITAT: WA (Jurien Bay to Albany). Woodland and heath in well drained or seasonally wet soil.

BRANCHING TIURNDIN *Tribonanthes longipetala*

SIZE/ID: Leaves to 18cm x 4mm, erect, green/brown. Infl. 6–30cm tall, 1–7-flowered, upper part of stem woolly. Flowers 20–30mm across, white or cream, occas. purplish. Tepals spreading widely, woolly. Stamens yellow. FLOWERING: Jul–Sep.
RANGE/HABITAT: WA (Moora to Albany). Seasonally wet flats and granite outcrops.

GOLDEN WEATHER GRASS

Hypoxis hygrometrica var. *hygrometrica*

SIZE/ID: Leaves grass-like, to 18cm x 1.5mm, dark green, hairy, flat or V-shaped in cross-section. Infl. 1–3, 2–20cm long, usually 1-flowered. Flowers 14–22mm across, bright yellow. NOTES: Roots are reportedly edible raw. FLOWERING: Aug–Jan. RANGE/HABITAT: NSW (s from Armidale), Vic, Tas, SA (se). Common in moist/wet grassy areas, but also drier habitats.

MONTANE WEATHER GRASS

Hypoxis hygrometrica var. *splendida*

SIZE/ID: Leaves to 18cm x 4mm, dark green, hairy, flat or V-shaped in cross-section. Infl. 1–3, 10–20cm long, usually 1-flowered. Flowers 10–25mm across, bright yellow. FLOWERING: Oct–Mar. RANGE/HABITAT: NSW (s from New England tlnd), Vic (ne). Mainly higher alt. in moist/wet grassy areas.

PALM LILY *Molineria capitulata*

Fruit.

SIZE/ID: Leaves palm-like on petiole to 80cm long, blade to 150 x 20cm, dark green, pleated/ribbed. Flowers in clustered heads to 5cm across at plant base, bracts brown, each flower 20–25mm across, yellow. Berries to 8 x 6mm, white with brown hairs, fleshy (sweet tasting). FLOWERING: Sporadic.
RANGE/HABITAT: Tropical Qld, NT (n). Rainforest.

TINY STAR *Pauridia glabella*

SIZE/ID: Leaves to 25cm x 1mm, dark green, channelled. Infl. 1–4, 2.5–20cm long, 1- or 2-flowered. Flowers 6–24mm across, bright yellow (occas. green externally), occas. setting seed without opening. FLOWERING: Aug–Mar.
RANGE/HABITAT: NSW, Vic, Tas, SA, WA. Common in moist/wet grassy areas, but also drier habitats.

QUADRI STAR *Pauridia occidentalis* var. *quadriloba*

SIZE/ID: Distinctive variant that can be immediately recognised by having only 4 tepals and 4 stamens. Flowers 12–20mm across, yellow, the tepals spreading widely like a cross. NOTES: A very distinctive and easily recognisable variety. FLOWERING: Aug–Dec. RANGE/HABITAT: WA (Geraldton to Esperance). Woodland and shrubland.

YELLOW STAR *Pauridia vaginata*

SIZE/ID: Leaves to 35cm x 2.5mm, dark green, channelled. Infl. 1–4, 6–35cm long, 1- or 2-flowered. Flowers 15–25mm across, bright yellow internally and externally. NOTES: Variable sp. FLOWERING: Aug–Mar.

RANGE/HABITAT: NSW, Vic, Tas, SA, WA. Common in moist/wet grassy areas, but also drier habitats.

TASMANIAN WHITE IRIS *Diplarrena latifolia*

SIZE/ID: Tall clumps. Leaves to 1m x 20mm, green to bluish. Scapes to 1.2m long. Spathes 6.5–8.5cm long, green, glabrous. Flowers 7–8.5cm across, white. Sepals to 4.2 x 3cm, spreading, white. Petals c.2.5cm long; hooding petal purple; projecting petals yellow, finely veined and tipped with purple. Capsules to 2.5cm long.
FLOWERING: Jan–Mar.
RANGE/HABITAT: Tas. Coast to mountains in wetter heath and moorland.

WHITE IRIS *Diplarrena moraea*

SIZE/ID: Tall narrow clumps. Leaves to 70cm x 10mm, green to bluish. Scapes to 1m long. Spathes 4–8cm long, green, glabrous. Flowers 5–7cm across, white. Sepals to 3.5 x 2.2cm, spreading, white. Petals 2–2.5cm long; hooding petal white; projecting petals mainly yellow, finely veined with grey/brown, white tipped. Capsules to 2.5cm long. NOTES: White flowers on tall scapes wave in the breeze. FLOWERING: Oct–Feb.
RANGE/HABITAT: NSW (se), Vic (e), Tas. Wetter forests and heath.

TASMANIAN PURPLESTAR *Isophysis tasmanica*

SIZE/ID: Endemic monotypic genus. Perennial with leaves in fans, each leaf to 30cm x 5mm, tough, glaucous, margins brown, papery. Scapes to 40cm tall. Flowers solitary, starry, 6–12cm across, usually dark purple or blackish, occas. yellow. Tepals 6, to 6cm x 9mm, veined, spreading widely or reflexed, pointed. Stamens 3, yellow. Capsule to 2cm long, veined. FLOWERING: Dec–Jan. RANGE/HABITAT: Tas (w and s). Coastal sedgeland and heath to alpine herbfield up to 1,300m alt.

GRASS FLAG *Libertia paniculata*

SIZE/ID: Dense spreading clumps. Leaves to 60cm x 12mm, erect, pale green. Panicles to 75cm long. Flowers 15–25mm across, white. Petals larger than sepals. Sepals to 8 x 3mm. Petals to 13 x 7mm. Anthers cream to brownish. Capsules to 8mm long. NOTES: Widespread and common. FLOWERING: Oct–Nov. RANGE/HABITAT: Qld (se), NSW, Vic (e). Wetter forests, gullies and stream banks.

WESTERN MORNING IRIS *Orthrosanthus laxus* var. *laxus*

SIZE/ID: Plants 20–55cm tall. Leaves to 45cm x 5mm, stiffly/rigidly erect, green. Panicles to 55cm long, few-branched. Buds enclosed in glassy bracts. Flowers 25–35mm across, blue. Stamens free. Anthers pale yellow. Capsules to 15mm long. FLOWERING: Aug–Oct.

RANGE/HABITAT: WA (Geraldton to Albany). Woodland and heath.

GRASS-LEAVED MORNING IRIS

Orthrosanthus laxus var. *gramineus*

SIZE/ID: Plants 20–35cm tall. Leaves to 35cm x 2mm, loose to spreading, pale green. Panicles to 40cm long, few-branched. Buds enclosed in glassy bracts. Flowers 20–30mm across, blue (often pale blue). Stamens free. Anthers cream to pale yellow.
FLOWERING: Aug–Oct.
RANGE/HABITAT: WA (Moora to Albany). Woodland and heath.

SOUTH STIRLING MORNING IRIS

Orthrosanthus muelleri

SIZE/ID: Plants 20–30cm tall. Leaves to 20cm x 2.5mm, erect, crowded, veins prominent, margins densely hairy. Panicles to 30cm long, few-branched. Buds enclosed in glassy bracts. Flowers 20–30mm across, bright blue. Stamens free. Anthers pale yellow. Capsules to 20mm long. FLOWERING: Sep–Oct.
RANGE/HABITAT: WA (Kamballup to Ongerup). Woodland and mallee heath in shallow sandy loam.

MORNING IRIS *Orthrosanthus multiflorus*

SIZE/ID: Plants 30–60cm tall. Leaves to 50cm x 6mm, erect, crowded, dark green, flat. Panicles to 60cm long, few-branched. Buds enclosed in glassy bracts. Flowers 20–30mm across, bright blue (rarely white), showy. Stamens united. Anthers orange/yellow. Capsules to 20mm long. FLOWERING: Sep–Dec.
RANGE/HABITAT: WA (Stirling Ra. to Israelite Bay), SA (Eyre Pen., Kangaroo Is.), Vic (sw). Heath and treed heath.

DWARF PURPLE FLAG *Patersonia babianoides*

SIZE/ID: Dwarf resprouting iris with a corm-like rhizome. Leaf usually solitary, occas. 2, petiolate, to 16cm x 12mm, green, pleated, hairy. Infl. basal, 2–4cm long. Floral bracts green, densely hairy. Flowers 3–4cm across, mauve/blue. Sepals to 2 x 1.5cm. Petals narrow. NOTES: Distinctive within the genus for its annual above-ground and below-ground regrowth, dwarf habit and soft, pleated, petiolate leaf. FLOWERING: Sep–Nov.
RANGE/HABITAT: WA (Darling Ra. to Mt Lindesay). Jarrah forest in sand, gravel and laterite.

SHORT PURPLE FLAG *Patersonia fragilis*

SIZE/ID: Clumps to 60cm tall. Leaves to 60cm x 6mm, terete, grooved, crowded, bluish or powdery, often sharply tipped. Scapes to 25cm long, glabrous. Spathes 2.5–4cm long, glabrous. Flowers 3–6cm across, violet to pale blue. Sepals to 2.3 x 1.5cm.
FLOWERING: Aug–Dec.
RANGE/HABITAT: Qld (se), NSW, Vic, Tas, SA. Open forest and moist/wet heath in sand.

LEAFY PURPLE FLAG *Patersonia glabrata*

SIZE/ID: Plants with erect lanky growths to 80cm tall. Leaves to 40cm x 5mm, flat, green, glabrous. Scapes to 25cm long, glabrous. Spathes 4–6.5cm long, striate, sparsely hairy. Flowers 4–6cm across, violet to pale blue. Sepals to 3 x 2.5cm. FLOWERING: Aug–Oct.

RANGE/HABITAT: Qld (n to Rockhampton), NSW, Vic (e). Open forest, woodland and coastal heath in sand.

NORTHERN PURPLE FLAG *Patersonia macrantha*

SIZE/ID: Clumps to 50cm tall. Leaves to 50cm x 9mm, flat, crowded, dark green to bluish. Scapes to 50cm long, glabrous. Spathes 4–7cm long, strongly veined, silky hairy. Flowers 6–8cm across, purple. Sepals to 4 x 3cm. NOTES: Flowers in the wet season. FLOWERING: Dec–Mar.

RANGE/HABITAT: Tropical NT (n, Melville Is.). Forest and woodland in sand and laterite.

LONG PURPLE FLAG

Patersonia occidentalis var. *occidentalis*

SIZE/ID: Clumps to 80cm tall. Leaves to 55cm x 10mm, flat, green, glabrous. Scapes to 80cm long, hairy. Spathes 2–6cm long, brown, glabrous. Flowers 4–7cm across, violet to purple. Sepals to 3.5 x 2.2cm. FLOWERING: Sep–Dec.

RANGE/HABITAT: Vic, Tas, SA, WA. Common in coastal/near-coastal forest, scrub and heath in wettish sites.

SILKY PURPLE FLAG *Patersonia sericea* var. *sericea*

SIZE/ID: Clumps to 50cm tall. Leaves to 50cm x 6mm, flat to terete, green, base and margins hairy. Scapes to 55cm long, hairy. Spathes 2–6cm long, veined, blackish, silky hairy. Flowers 4–6cm across, violet to purple. Sepals to 3 x 2.5cm. FLOWERING: Jun–Dec. RANGE/HABITAT: Qld (n to Rockhampton), NSW, Vic (e). Open forest and woodland in stony soil; coastal heath in sand.

YELLOW FLAG *Patersonia umbrosa* var. *xanthina*

SIZE/ID: Clumps to 1m tall. Leaves erect, to 90cm x 10mm, crowded, flat, dark green, glabrous. Scapes to 80cm long, glabrous. Spathes 6–8.5cm long, green, glabrous. Flowers 5–7cm across, bright yellow. Sepals to 3.5 x 2.5cm. FLOWERING: Aug–Oct. RANGE/HABITAT: WA (Darling Ra. to Deep R.). Winter-wet sites in jarrah and karri forest in sand and laterite.

NORTHERN STREAM LILY *Helmholtzia acorifolia*

SIZE/ID: Clumps 1–2m tall. Leaves to 1.5m x 4cm, dark green, shiny, leathery, midrib prominent, tapered to long point. Panicles to 2m long, woolly. Flowers white, crowded. Sepals 8–14mm long. Petals 3mm long. Stamen 4mm long. Anthers bright yellow. Fruit indehiscent, hairy. NOTES: Often in colonies with seedlings germinating on rocks, banks and rotting logs. FLOWERING: Jul–Oct. RANGE/HABITAT: Qld (ne). Streambanks and swamps in highland rainforest.

STREAM LILY *Helmholtzia glaberrima*

SIZE/ID: Clumps to 1.5m tall. Leaves to 50cm x 7cm, dark green, shiny, leathery, tapered to long point. Panicles to 1m long, glabrous, top of scape with numerous bracts. Flowers pale pink to deep pink, crowded. Sepals c.8mm long. Petals 4–5mm long. Stamen 4.5mm long. Anthers bright yellow. Capsule 5–7mm long. FLOWERING: Sep–Apr. AKA *Orthothylax glaberrima*.
RANGE/HABITAT: Qld, NSW (McPherson Ra. to Mt Warning). Streambanks and steep slopes in rainforest.

BLUE HYACINTH *Pontederia cyanea*

SIZE/ID: Aquatic plant. Stems to 40cm long. Leaves to 18 x 8cm, spreading, bright green, shiny; petiole swollen, blade ovate. Racemes to 8cm long, 3–15-flowered. Flowers 25–40mm across, brilliant blue. Stamens clustered, yellow. Capsules 10–15mm long. NOTES: Often in spreading patches. FLOWERING: mainly Jan–May, also sporadic.
RANGE/HABITAT: Qld, NSW, NT, WA. Swamps, lagoons and sluggish streams in mud or water to 1m deep.

SMALL SUPPLEJACK *Ripogonum fawcettianum*

SIZE/ID: Climber. Stems to 4m tall, rusty hairy, with or without prickles. Leaves opposite, to 10 x 3.5cm, spreading, dark green and shiny above, whitish beneath. Racemes axillary. Flowers crowded, 8–10mm across, cream, white or pinkish with large pinkish stamens. Petals slightly larger than sepals. Berries 8–12mm across, orange/red. FLOWERING: Jun–Sep.
RANGE/HABITAT: Qld, NSW (McPherson Ra. to Gosford). Rainforest.

TALL YELLOW-EYE *Xyris operculata*

SIZE/ID: Plants in tufts. Leaves to 60cm x 1mm, grass-like, green; sheathing base reddish brown to blackish, shiny. Scapes 60–90cm long, stiff. Infl. c.1 x 1cm, a cluster of bracts widest near apex. Bracts brown, margins fringed. Flowers 10–20mm across, yellow, 3-petalled, each flower lasting less than a day. FLOWERING: Oct–Feb.

RANGE/HABITAT: Qld, NSW, Tas, SA. Moist to wet heathland and swamps.

CAPE YORK LILY, NATIVE TURMERIC

Curcuma australasica

SIZE/ID: Rhizome yellow inside. Leaves tufted; petiole to 15cm long; blades to 45 x 19cm, bright green, veined. Infl. to 15cm long, cylindrical, with large overlapping, concave bracts curving outwards. Flowers 1.5–2cm long, tubular, yellow (rarely white), exserted from the lower green fertile bracts. Upper bracts sterile in a terminal crown, bright pink. NOTES: Roots can be used in cooking and eaten roasted. FLOWERING: Nov–Mar.
RANGE/HABITAT: Tropical Qld, NT; also NG. Rainforest margins.

Crinum pedunculatum,
Jervis Bay, NSW. S. Jones.

GLOSSARY

Actinomorphic: Regularly symmetrical; a flower which can be divided equally in more than one plane.

Amaryllid: Group name applied to plants of the family Amaryllidaceae.

Anther: The pollen-bearing part of a stamen.

Aroid: Group name applied to plants of the family Araceae.

Berry: A fleshy many-seeded fruit that does not split when ripe.

Bisexual: Both male and female sexes present.

Bulb: A storage organ consisting of fleshy scales attached to a basal plate.

Bulbil: Vegetative seed-like or bulb-like structures that are genetically identical to the parent.

Bulbous: Swollen and fleshy like a bulb.

Capsule: A dry fruit that splits open to release seeds.

Cladode: Green photosynthetic stem acting as a leaf.

Clonal: Vegetative propagation.

Clone: Genetically identical plants arising from clonal propagation.

Compound leaf: A leaf with two or more separate leaflets.

Corm: A storage organ consisting of solid tissue (no scales or baseplate).

Cormous: Bearing a corm.

Corona: A crown-like central growth found in the flowers of many Amaryllids.

Dioecious: Bearing male and female flowers on separate plants.

Evergreen: Remaining green and retaining leaves throughout the year.

Family: A taxonomic group of related genera.

Filament: The stalk of a stamen that supports the anther.

Genus: A taxonomic group of closely related species.

Glabrous: Without hairs.

Glaucous: Bluish to bluish grey.

Indehiscent: Not splitting open at maturity.

Inflorescence (infl.): The flowering structure of a plant (the supporting flower stem and the flowers).

Irid: Group name applied to plants of the family Iridaceae.

Leaflet: Segment of a compound leaf.

Linear: Long and narrow with parallel sides.

Littoral: Growing on the shores of a lake, sea or ocean.

Mallee: A eucalypt with multiple stems arising from at or below ground level; also a habitat dominated by mallee trees.

Monocotyledon: Angiosperm plant with a single seed leaf and parallel leaf venation.

Monoecious: Bearing separate male and female flowers on the same plant.

Occluded: Closed together or joined.

Panicle: A branched infl.

Perennial: Plant lasting several years.

Perianth: A collective term for all the sepals and petals of a flower.

Petal: A segment of the inner perianth whorl of a flower.

Petiole: The stem or stalk of a leaf.

Pseudostem: False stem formed by the overlapping/fused fleshy leaf bases of some large evergreen bulbs.

Raceme: Unbranched infl. with stalked flowers.

Rachis: The main axis of a compound leaf or infl.

Resprouting: Plants that die back to a storage organ to avoid hot, dry conditions.

GLOSSARY

Rhizome: An underground stem.

Scape: Flower stem.

Sepal: A segment of the calyx or outer perianth whorl of a flower.

Sessile: Without a stalk.

Spadix: The fleshy spike in an aroid infl. that contains small sunken flowers.

Spathe: Leathery/papery/flimsy bract that encloses flowers or an inflorescence; in aroids it is the bract that encloses the spadix.

Species: A group of closely related plants with a common set of features that sets them apart from another species.

Subequal: Not equal; as in tepals when the inner whorl and outer whorl are slightly different.

Subspecies: A taxonomic subgroup within a species used to differentiate geographically isolated variants.

Spike: Unbranched infl. with sessile flowers.

Sucker: A shoot arising from the roots below ground level.

Tepals: Term used when sepals and petals are of similar shape, size and colour.

Terete: Slender and cylindrical.

Terminal: At the end.

Trifoliolate: Compound leaf with three leaflets.

Tuberous: Swollen and fleshy.

Umbel: Flat- or curve-topped umbrella-like inflorescence.

Unisexual: Of one sex only, either male or female.

Vegetative: Asexual growth or propagation.

Whorl: More than two organs arising from the one place.

Zygomorphic: Said of a flower with only one plane of symmetry.

ABRS/CSIRO. 2011. *Flora of Australia*, Volume 39, Alismatales to Arales. Melbourne.

Australian Government Publishing Service. 1986. *Flora of Australia*, Volume 46, Iridaceae to Dioscoreaceae. Canberra.

Australian Government Publishing Service. 1987. *Flora of Australia* Volume 45, Hydatellaceae to Liliaceae. Canberra.

Barrett, R L, and Dixon, K W. 2001. A revision of *Calectasia* (Calectasiaceae) with eight new species described from south-west Western Australia. *Nuytsia* 13(3): 411–488.

Barrett, R.L. and Barrett, M.D. (2015). Twenty-seven new species of vascular plants from Western Australia. *Nuytsia* 26: 21–87.

Bates, R.J. (1995). The species of *Wurmbea* (Liliaceae) in South Australia. *J. Adel. Bot. Gard.* 16: 33–53.

Bates, R.J. (1995). A review of South Australian *Wurmbea* (Colchicaceae-Liliaceae); keys, new taxa and combinations, and notes. *J. Adel. Bot. Gard.* 21: 75–81.

Hay, A. (1993). The genus *Typhonium* (Araceae-Areae) in Australasia, *Blumea* 37: 345–376.

Hay, A, Barrett, M D, and Hetterscheid, W L A. 2022. New combinations in a resurrected *Lazarum* A. Hay (Araceae-Areae). *Aroideana* 45(3): 133–137.

Horsfall, P F, and Albrecht, D E. 2020. *Bulbine fraseri* (Asphodelaceae) reinstated and distinguished from *B. bulbosa* (R.Br.) Haw. in eastern Australia. *Austrobaileya* 10(4): 612–620.

Keighery, G J. 2001. A new species of *Chamaescilla* (Anthericaceae) from Western Australia. *Nuytsia* 13(3): 475–478.

Keighery, G J, and Muir, W. 2005. Reinstatement of *Burchardia congesta* (Colchicaceae). *Nuytsia* 15(3): 347–353.

FURTHER READING

Lang, P J. 2008. *Calostemma abdicatum* (Amaryllidaceae), a new species of Garland Lily endemic to the Everard Ranges, and a comparison of the three species within *Calostemma* R.Br. *J. Adel. Bot. Gard.* 22: 47–56.

Lehmiller, D J, Lykos, J R, and Hamilton, R. 2012a. The enigma of *Crinum uniflorum* F. Muell. (Amaryllidaceae) and the justification for two new Australian *Crinum* species. *Herbertia* 66: 89–119.

Lehmiller, D J, Lykos, J R, and Hamilton, R. 2012b. New *Crinum* taxa from Australia. *Herbertia* 66: 120–145.

Macfarlane, T D, and van Leeuwen, S J. 1996. *Wurmbea saccata* (Colchicaceae), a lepidopteran-pollinated new species from Western Australia. *Nuytsia* 10(3): 429–435.

Macfarlane, T D, and Case, A L. 2007. *Wurmbea inflata* (Colchicaceae), a new species from the Gascoyne Region of Western Australia. *Nuytsia* 17: 223–228.

Macfarlane, T D, and Case, A L. 2011. *Wurmbea fluviatilis* (Colchicaceae), a new riverine species from the Gascoyne Region of Western Australia. *Nuytsia* 21(1): 25–30.

McLay, T G B, and Bayly, M J. 2016. A new family placement for Australian blue squill, *Chamaescilla*: Xanthorrhoeaceae (Hemerocallidoideae), not Asparagaceae. *Phytotaxa* 275(2): 97–111.

Morris, D I, and Duretto, M F. 2005. A new species of *Bulbine* (Asphodelaceae) from Wilsons Promontory and islands of eastern Bass Strait. *Muelleria* 22: 93–96.

Simpson, J, Conran, J G, Biffin, E, van Dijk, K-J, and Waycott, M. 2022. The *Crinum flaccidum* (Amaryllidaceae) species complex in Australia. *Aust. Syst. Bot.* 35(5): 395–402.

INDEX

INDEX

OTHER TITLES IN THE SERIES

Animals of Australia
Ken Stepnell ISBN 978 1 92151 754 9

Birds of Australia
Ken Stepnell ISBN 978 1 92151 753 2

Butterflies of Australia
Paul Zborowski ISBN 978 1 92554 694 1

Ferns of Australia
David L Jones ISBN 978 1 76079 634 1

Frogs of Australia
Marion Anstis ISBN 978 1 92151 790 7

Insects of Australia
Paul Zborowski ISBN 978 1 92554 644 6

Snakes of Australia
Gerry Swan ISBN 978 1 92151 789 1

Spiders of Australia
Volker W Framenau and Melissa L Thomas
ISBN 978 1 92554 603 3

Trees of Australia
David L Jones ISBN 978 1 92554 688 0

Wild Flowers of Australia
Ken Stepnell ISBN 978 1 92151 755 6

For details of these books and hundreds of other Natural History titles see newhollandpublishers.com